12/11

CR

D0555833

THE BEGINNINGS OF FARMING

At about the same time as the founding of the first civilizations (c.5000 BCE) mankind also developed the art of cultivating crops. The annual flooding of the river valleys where these first civilizations were established deposited a rich silt on the surrounding land, as happened with the Nile allowing the early Egyptians to cultivate their valley.

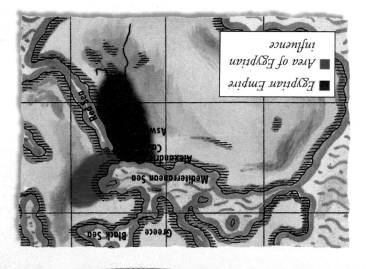

A KINGDOM UNITED

Originally, Egypt was divided into two kingdoms, Upper and Lower Egypt. They were united under Pharaoh Menes in c.3100 BCE, who founded the I dynasty. The period known as the Old Kingdom lasted from the III to the VI dynasty. The New Kingdom period (c.1550-1070 BCE) saw an age of great military expansion, from Nubia in the south to the Euphrates River in the east.

SIGN OF LIFE

This libation dish is in the form of an ankh cross. The ankh was the Egyptian symbol for life. Only the king, his queen or the gods were allowed to carry it.

THE FIRST WRITING

The first known system of writing appeared in Sumeria, north-east of Egypt, around 3200 BCE, in the form of simple pictograms. The Egyptians developed this into an incredibly complex system of writing called hieroglyphs, using over 700 different symbols. The symbols expressed ideas rather than words and were used mostly for sacred writings.

MONUMENTAL BUILDINGS

The Egyptians built pyramids, huge funerary monuments, to house the bodies of their dead kings (pharaohs). The king was buried with precious goods to take on his journey into the afterlife. The Great Pyramid of Khufu (Cheops) at Giza (shown above) was built c.2551 BCE. After about 2150 BCE pyramids were no longer built and kings were buried in subterranean rock tombs.

Life for the Rich

With the passage of over 6,000 years it is very difficult for us today to obtain a complete picture about everyday life in ancient Egypt. As is the case for all societies at any period in the past, what remains are the belongings of the wealthy and, more especially, royalty. While the magnificent buildings, art and artefacts tell us a great deal about the sophistication and wealth of the wealthy and, more especially, royalty. While the magnificent buildings, art and artefacts tell us very little about what life was like for ordinary people. Most of the hieroglyphs and scripts speak of government and ritual. Although much of our understanding of the lower orders of their society must remain speculative, at least we can be fairly certain that wealthier Egyptians and nobles enjoyed an opulent lifestyle. Comfort and hygiene featured strongly in their lives. They had strong family values and most wealthy households employed servants or slaves to carry out the mundane tasks.

ORNATE FURNITURE

Wood was in short supply in Egypt, but the wealthy could afford exotic imports, such as Lebanese cedar or ebony. Carpenters were skilled craftsmen and decorated their work with fine inlays and friezes, as seen in this chair.

ORNAMENTAL GLASS

The arts of glass-making and enameling were well known to the Egyptians. They also made fine white and colored porcelain of a comparable quality to that made in China. Houses of the wealthy were decorated with many fine art piece such as this beautiful glass perfume bottle in the shape of a bulti fish.

CONTENTS

Who were the Ancient Egyptians?

FIRST INDUSTRY

The technique of extracting metal ores from rock was developed in about 4500 BCE in both Egypt and Sumeria, which enabled more durable tools and weapons to be made. The metal workers shown here are smelting copper.

ometime around 5000 BCE, mankind organized itself into city-states, the first true civilizations. The process appears to have occurred simultaneously, but quite independently, at different sites across the world. What caused this change in humanity's basic character from a nomadic to a settled existence we shall probably never know. Nor the precise date it occurred. All we do know is based upon physical remains excavated so far; other sites, older still perhaps, may still await discovery. All of these early civilizations were centered on major river valleys: the Yellow River in China; the Indus River in India; the Tigris-Euphrates in the Middle East and the Nile in Egypt. The Egyptian civilization, although probably not the oldest, grew to become, perhaps, the greatest of these ancient cultures.

THE POTTER'S ART

The Egyptians invented the potter's wheel, sometime around 4000 BCE. Before that, pots were fashioned by hand pressing wet clay into shapes and leaving to dry.

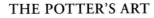

CIVILIZATIONS

THE HISTORY OF THE ANCIENT WORLD

ticktock

FINE JEWELRY

Egyptian jewelry was striking in the originality of its design. Skilled metalworkers fashioned all manner of shapes by welding thin strips of metal into intricate designs using molten sulfur. Gold (beaten or molded) and fine jewels, such as turquoise and amethyst, were commonly used. They were embellished with fine ceramics and painted glass which, to the Egyptians, were almost as expensive as semi-precious stones.

KEEPING UP APPEARANCES

Most Egyptians took a pride in their appearance, especially the wealthy who could afford the finest materials. Both men and women had their hair cut short, but wore elaborately braided and decorated wigs. The wealthier they were, the more elaborate their headdresses were, such as a gold headband decorated with semi-precious stones, as seen here. Both sexes seem also to have used cosmetics, in particular eye make-up.

SPACIOUS HOUSES

The houses of the rich were quite large, often occupying two stories, and were made from bricks covered in white painted plaster. They were raised on platforms as protection against damp— as shown on this papyrus. Most also had a small, shady garden with an ornamental pool. Inside they were highly decorated with frescoes and enameled wall paintings.

COMFORTABLE LIFESTYLE

Houses were quite comfortably, if simply, furnished, making great use of rare woods and fabrics imported from abroad. Most furniture was quite elaborately carved, such as lion-claw feet on tables and chairs. Beds, complete with stuffed mattresses, also had head and foot rests and reclining back boards. The wooden head rest shown here was probably used for resting during the day.

Life for the Poor

Although life for the poor was hard in ancient Egypt, by comparison to other societies of the time, even they had a reasonably high standard of living. Most peasants worked in the fields, while many others were employed in the massive building programs of the pharaohs. Most were well treated. A stable family life was important to all classes of Egyptians. Great respect was accorded to elderly relatives. Once children became teenagers they often became servants to more affluent families. Houses, whether in town or country, were constructed of dried mud, mixed with straw and made into bricks. They were reasonably spacious, usually two stories, with flat roofs in which a vent was provided to catch the cool north winds.

TIMELESS SCENE

Over 90% of Egypt is desert. Virtually the only fertile region capable of supporting life, apart from small oases, was along the flood plains of the River Nile. This modern picture shows an almost timeless agricultural scene in Egypt. Many of the farming techniques practiced today have hardly changed since ancient times.

GETTING ABOUT

Few poor people could afford wagons, horses or camels to transport themselves and their goods about. The most common form of transport for them was donkeys. There were few proper roads so transport was always difficult. For many people the only journeys they ever undertook were to and from the local market. Donkeys still provide the main means of transport for poor Egyptians in remote areas today.

BASIC ACCOMMODATION

This clay model shows a typical poor Egyptian's house with an arched doorway and small windows to keep the heat out. Known as a "soul house," the model would have been buried with its owner to take into the next life.

A MEASURE OF WEALTH

The measure of a man's wealth was calculated by the number of beasts he owned, such as goats and geese, but particularly cattle. Scribes recorded the details and people were taxed accordingly. The agricultural season in ancient Egypt (as it still was until the construction of the Aswan dam in the 1960s) was governed by the annual flooding of the Nile. Each year the river burst its banks, depositing a thick black silt over a considerable distance of the surrounding land making it very fertile. Farmers also constructed irrigation channels from the river far into their fields to grow more crops inland.

SLAVE TRADE

Although the ancient Egyptians did extend their rule over a small empire in north Africa and the eastern Mediterranean, they were not by nature a war-like people. When they did make forays into other lands, such as Nubia, Ethiopia or Lebanon, they captured native peoples and brought them back to Egypt as slaves. Some were put to work as servants in rich households, but mostly they provided the labor for the almost continuous building programmes of the pharaohs.

HARD LABOR

This wall painting from the Sennudem tomb in Thebes dates from *c.*1200 BCE and shows farming practices at about that time. An ox is used to pull a rather primitive wooden plow. The plowman is using a whip, made from papyrus, to swat flies and drive on the ox.

SPICE OF LIFE

Egypt was at the center of the known world and all major trade routes passed through it, bringing exotic foods and spices from the East. Banquets could be exceptionally lavish with a variety of meats, fruit, vegetables, poultry and eggs.

VINTAGE WINE

The Egyptians grew grapes both as a table dessert and for making wine. Wine was usually only drunk by the rich. The more common alcoholic drink was beer, made from barley. It had a thick consistency and was drunk through a syphon.

A SWEETENER

To sweeten their foods, Egyptians generally used either fruits, such as dates mashed down, or honey. Bees were kept in conical pottery hives, as shown here. They were thought of as small birds rather than as insects.

FAMILY AFFAIR

This detail from a stucco wall painting comes from the tomb of Sennedjem and shows the tomb owner and his wife working in the fields. There was no centrally organized system of agriculture and

each family produced its own food, taking any excess to market. The Egyptians are believed to have invented the first ox-drawn plow, about 3100 BCE.

Food & Drink

Most Egyptians seem to have eaten very well, though they did suffer periodic plagues of insects (such as locusts) that destroyed crops and caused famine. Their agricultural methods were somewhat primitive (given the sophistication of their society as a whole) and most practiced a subsistence form of farming, growing just sufficient for their needs. Nevertheless, the average Egyptian was able to choose from a wide variety of foods, including various meats, fish, vegetables (such as onions, leeks, turnips, and garlic) and fruits (including grapes, figs, dates, and pomegranates). They also perfected the technique of artificially incubating chickens to ensure plentiful supplies of poultry. Wine was a great favorite, particularly with the wealthy, and was made from both grapes and dates. During the 7th century, Egypt had a sudden influx of Arabs, which changed many of the fundamental ways of life. Islam became the official religion, and as Muslims are not allowed to drink alcohol, the production of wine and beer went into decline.

THE BUTCHER'S TRADE

Wealthy Egyptians enjoyed a variety of meats, including sheep, oxen, poultry and wild animals, such as antelope, as shown here. Butchers often gave part of the slaughtered animals as religious sacrifices. Poorer people could not afford much meat and usually caught fish as a freely available substitute.

OPEN HEARTHS

Cooking was usually done in clay ovens or open charcoal fires, as shown here. The kitchen was often located outside, away from the living rooms, to avoid the risk of fires and reduce smells.

The boy in this wooden sculpture is fanning a fire in preparation to cook the duck in his hand.

ROUGHAGE

The Egyptian diet contained plenty of fiber as flour used in bread-making was only coarsely ground. Bread, made from barley and wheat, formed the staple diet of many Egyptians. Loaves were placed into flat round molds. Bakers also made a variety of cakes using fruits such as figs or dates.

Pastimes

ost of the evidence so far gleaned about everyday life in ancient Egypt would seem to indicate that, certainly at its apex, around the time of the XVIII and XIX dynasties (*c.*1550-1196 BCE) life was generally good for most people. They spent a high proportion of their time in the pursuit of leisure, which is normally indicative of a wealthy society. Those people from poorer societies are usually too preoccupied with the essentials of life, such as providing food and shelter. Not so, the Egyptians. Their society was refined and orderly, which is reflected in the nature of their pastimes. Many of them are family or solitary pursuits. They did not appear to engage in large-scale public entertainment, such as the theater or stadiums, as did the Greeks and Romans.

GYPSIES

Modern-day gypsies
may not be descended
from eastern Europeans,
as is sometimes suggested,
but from Egyptians who fled
their homeland at the time
of the Greek occupation.
Many traditional gypsy
pastimes, like horse racing and
communal singing and dancing,
may also have been practiced
in ancient Egypt.

EXOTIC DANCING

A popular pastime in the
king's palace, or at banquets
held by the rich, was song and
dance. Servant girls undertook
rigorous dance training and
they performed, sometimes
naked, alongside
gymnasts and jugglers
while musicians
played. Dancing also often
accompanied religious
ceremonies.

THE FIRST HARP

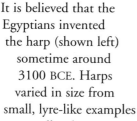

It is believed that the Egyptians invented the harp (shown left) sometime around 3100 BCE. Harps varied in size from small, lyre-like examples to ones taller than a man, the hollow chamber usually made out of wood. Other early instruments included the flute, made from hollow reeds, bronze cymbals, and tambourines.

SENET

This senet board is intricately made from wood and contains a drawer to house the playing pieces. The board is divided into 30 squares and dates from about 1200 BCE.

BOARD GAMES

Board games were very popular with the Egyptians. The most popular was senet, in which two players tried to reach the kingdom of the gods. In the example left, the board has been drawn onto a papyrus sheet. Other games, more familiar today, were backgammon and chess. One of the oldest games ever discovered was "snake," in which players moved pieces around a spiral board to the snake's head in the center.

FAMILY VALUES

Egyptian society, at all levels, placed great store in family values. Families were quite large, with between 8 and 12 children. Though children were expected to work, there was still plenty of time for play. Egyptians were great storytellers and everyone gathered round to hear the father recite tales of the gods and of heroic exploits.

HEADDRESS

It was fashionable for men and women to wear either wigs, made from human hair and held in place by beeswax, or headdresses. These might take the form of elaborate hats with stiffened collars made of fine material, or resemble wigs, with finely braided hair and decorated with jewels. For the poorer classes, working in the fierce Egyptian sun, skull caps or bonnets sufficed.

Fashion

ll Egyptians liked to adorn their bodies with brightly painted cosmetics or jewelry, even the poorer classes, who simply used cheaper materials. Personal appearance and hygiene seem to have been very important to them and they were surprisingly fashion-conscious. Egypt was at the center of most of the trade routes to the Mediterranean and the East and new materials brought back from countries such as India were quickly bought up. Because of the hot climate, most clothes were simple, light and loose fitting. Men usually wore only a kilt or even just a loin cloth. Women wore skirts or dresses, similar to Indian saris. Many women are known to have gone topless and nudity was common amongst children up to the age of 12.

HAIRSTYLES

Most men and women had their hair cut short. They favored the use of wigs, or hair extensions fastened with hair pins made of wood or bone. Finely toothed combs made of wood or, as shown here, ivory, were used to create elaborate hairstyles on the wigs.

FOOTWEAR

This picture shows the production of papyrus, used to make a wide range of objects, including shoes. Occasionally shoes were made of leather, but most footwear consisted of simple sandals made from papyrus reeds. They were cheap to make and easily replaced, favored by people of all classes, including royalty and priests.

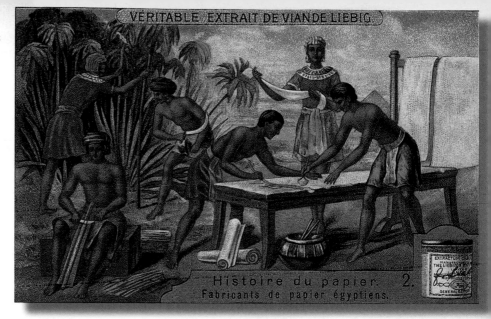

VÉRITABLE EXTRAIT DE VIANDE LIEBIG

Histoire du papier. 2.
Fabricants de papier égyptiens.

BODY BEAUTIFUL

Cosmetics were widely used and held in elaborately carved containers, such as shown above. Various minerals (some poisonous) were ground up to form pastes. Green eye shadow, made from malachite, was a favorite amongst men and women.

ADORNMENTS

Poorer people wore jewelry, such as rings and bracelets made of cheap metals and decorated with pieces of brightly painted clay. The wealthy made great use of gold and precious stones, freely available from the East. Metalworkers became very skilled at making jewelry by fashioning strips of metal into elaborate shapes, or by casting. This gold and lapis lazuli necklace (left) and scarab pectoral (right) came from the tomb of Tutankhamen.

PLEATED DRESS

Women usually wore long, loose fitting dresses, often made out of one piece of material and pleated. The over-tunic shown here is believed to be the oldest surviving garment in the world and dates from about 3000 BCE.

Art & Architecture

O ne of the most striking things about the remains of ancient Egypt is the monumental scale of its architecture. Whilst not in any way detracting from the skills of the masons responsible, not everything is as it first seems. Many of the huge monuments were not so much constructed as carved out of solid rock; an incredible feat in itself, of course, but one relating more perhaps to art than to architecture. The Sphinx at Giza, for example, was created in this way, as were many of the monolithic statues and entrance portals of the temples. Even the Great Pyramid contains an immense mound of natural bedrock at its core. We know much of everyday life in ancient Egypt from the engravings and reliefs etched into temple walls and pillars. The angular form of these carvings is very different from the huge statues, which were executed with perfect perspective; a remarkable achievement considering their great height. The Egyptians created many fine works of art, including wall paintings, statues, pottery and jewelry, but they saw them as intrinsic parts of life itself and not separate objects.

MONUMENTAL ART

Most of the more significant works of art and architecture to survive are from temples and tombs. Built on a grand scale, they are not representative of ancient Egyptian society as a whole. Monumental works on such a scale were never attempted again, not even in classical Greece and Rome. This view shows King Ramesses the Great at Luxor.

ARTISTIC LICENCE

Art was seen as an essentia part of architecture, and indeed of life itself. It told a story and attempted to place everything in a natural order. Accompanyi texts and hieroglyphs explained what the artist was trying to convey.

TEMPLE OF ABU SIMBEL

Ramesses II was something of an egoist and revived the colossal style of architectural building that had somewhat gone out of fashion amongst his predecessors. He constructed numerous huge statues of himself throughout Egypt. At Abu Simbel, in the Upper Nile, he built an impressive temple to himself and three gods (Amun, Re-Harakhty and Ptah). It is fronted by four huge statues of himself.

OBELISKS

Obelisks are tall, squared monoliths with pointed tops. They were usually placed in pairs at the entrance to temples. Hieroglyphs carved on their sides reflected who built them and to which deity they were dedicated. This one, along with the colossal statues of Ramesses II are to be seen at Luxor.

TEMPLE OF KARNAK

The Egyptians never mastered the use of arches. Instead, they roofed their immense buildings with huge flat slabs or corbelling, a series of slabs, each built out from the one below in decreasing steps until the gap was closed. This view shows the temple at Karnak, built by Ramesses II.

THE PYRAMIDS

The great pyramids of Giza were built as tombs for mighty Egyptian pharoahs. The Great Pyramid (right) was built around 2551 BCE to house the body of King Khufu. His mummified body was entombed in a secret chamber to safeguard against grave robbers, along with treasures for him to take into the afterlife. Despite hidden entrances and blocked-off passageways, Khufu's tomb was still looted and the robber's tunnel is now the main entrance. Built with phenomenal precision, it stands some 481 feet (146.6 meters) high, contains about 2,300,000 blocks of stone, and the base is level to within less than an inch (2.1cm).

King's chamber with stress relieving chambers above

Air shafts

Air shafts

Queen's chamber

Grand gallery

Subterranean chamber

Entrance

Descending passage

Mortuary temple

N

Queens' pyramids

Causeway

EMBALMING

Embalmers, although skilled in anatomy, were not doctors. They understood the causes of decay in bodies and so removed all of the internal organs, and pumped a bituminous substance into the body to preserve it for its journey into the afterlife. Incredibly, the brain was removed through the nostrils!

DOCTOR PRIESTS

In the early years of their civilization, the Egyptians saw disease as the result of an invasion of the body by evil spirits. Until physicians were allowed to practice medicine, only priests were permitted to cure the sick who would come to the temples such as this one at Edfou for treatment.

ANATOMY

Because Egyptians believed in an afterlife, doctors were forbidden to dissect human corpses. They had to rely on the dissection and examination of animals for their understanding of anatomy. They understood that the heart was the center of the circulatory system and the various functions of the organs within the body, including the brain.

Health & Medicine

The ancient Egyptians possessed considerable medical skills. Surviving texts also reveal that they had a surprisingly accurate knowledge of human anatomy. Nevertheless, medical treatment was a strange mixture of magic and science. Physicians and magicians often worked together to concoct potions to ward off evil spirits. Many ailments were thought to be caused by worm-like creatures that had to be purged from the body. Many of their herbal cures such as garlic, used in cooking and as a medicine, are still widely used today. Magical charms in the form of amulets were worn as protection against disease, and votive offerings or sacrifices were made to the gods. Because Egyptians believed in an afterlife, they did not believe ill-health was confined to the living so they buried magical charms with the deceased as protection in the underworld. Life expectancy was generally high and many Egyptians lived to age 80 and beyond.

DENTISTRY

This relief comes from the tomb of Hesire, chief dentist and physician to the king, and dates from c.2700 BCE. Studies of mummified bodies have revealed quite sophisticated dentistry skills. Egyptian doctors were not general practitioners, but each specialized in a particular part of the body.

NATIONAL HEALTH

The Greek historian Diodorus Siculus observed that the State of Egypt paid doctors' wages, allowing them to treat people free-of-charge during wartime or on any journey within Egypt. Priests in particular had to keep themselves free of disease and had to observe strict codes of cleanliness, including having their heads completely shaved as shown here.

PURE AIR

Breathing the scent of the sacred lotus flower was thought to be a protection against disease. Egyptians knew of the healing properties of several plants, such as hemlock and opium, which they made into ointments and gargles.

Love & Marriage

LEGENDARY LOVE

There is some evidence to suggest that incestuous relationships between brother and sister were sometimes allowed in ancient Egypt, usually amongst royalty. In religion, the sky goddess Nut was married to her brother, the earth god Geb, seen above.

Ordinary people in Egyptian society lived a comparatively relaxed lifestyle in which there was much time for enjoyment and socializing. After about the age of 12, children were regarded as young adults and could marry; especially girls, whose career prospects were more limited than boys. After marriage, men's obligations were to provide for their own family; the responsibility of looking after elderly parents fell to the women. Although priests were expected to devote their lives to the gods and carry out their duties on behalf of the pharaoh, they occupied a very high place in the social hierarchy and were allowed to marry and have families. They benefited from a very privileged form of inheritance which allowed them to acquire vast riches and land, which they held collectively as a priesthood. Priests' sons were allowed to inherit this great wealth and enjoyed a very exalted position in society.

GODDESS OF FERTILITY

The Egyptian goddess of fertility was Taweret, usually shown as a pregnant hippopotamus. Taweret is often depicted with a fierce countenance to ward off evil during childbirth. Women said prayers and made votive offerings to her during their pregnancy. In general, however, hippos were normally regarded as evil, especially the males, which were seen as the enemies of the gods Osiris and Horus.

FAMILY VIRTUES

By all accounts ancient Egyptians were a gentle people who observed many social graces. Single girls of high rank were chaperoned on their meetings with men and many marriages were arranged between both sets of parents to facilitate a better match, or to secure an income or inheritance. This was especially true for women, who seldom had an income of their own.

GIRL POWER

Ancient Egypt was very much a patriarchial society, though women married to important nobles could exert a great deal of influence behind the scenes. Sometimes wives at court would gather together, under the protection of the goddess Hathar, and petition their husbands. This devoted couple probably remained married throughout their lives, as was normal in high society; the heavy wigs denote their wealth. Women did not give up their acquired status easily.

DEVOTED COUPLE

Unlike other Middle-Eastern societies, ancient Egyptians were largely monogamous (men were only allowed one wife at a time) though some of the pharaohs and nobles may have had more. Apparently, it was very easy for people of all classes to obtain an annulment of their marriage. This *stela* (a kind of religious inscription placed inside a tomb, like a gravestone) shows a devoted couple who share the same grave and presumably hoped to travel to the afterlife together.

WEDDING CEREMONY

This wall painting shows a Nubian called Sennufer marrying his bride. They are being blessed with holy water by the high priest, using a sacred container called a *situla*. Brides often wore sacred lotus blossoms in their hair for good luck, or delicately perfumed pomanders fastened to their brocaded wigs.

Women & Children

Although ancient Egyptian society was dominated by men (few positions of power or authority were given to women), women nevertheless played an important role in providing a stable family environment. Only the wealthy could afford servants or slaves to perform menial tasks. For most families the responsibility of looking after the house, caring for the children, cooking and cleaning rested with the women. There were few professions open to women. Most doctors and priests were men, though occasionally a woman of high rank might become a priestess. However, male dominance was more by custom than by law.

CHILDREN'S GAMES

These carvings show children carrying models in the shape of birds. These would have been floated on water in much the same way as model boats are used today. Many modern games can be traced back to Egyptian times, including leap frog, piggy-back and tug-of-war.

CLEOPATRA

Egypt was overrun by invaders several times from about 1000 BCE on, including by the Greeks, under Alexander the Great. Cleopatra VII (shown above), although of Greek descent, was the last in the long line of rulers of Egypt. Unusually for a woman, she ruled in her own right. She embarked on a disastrous love-affair with the Roman general, Mark Anthony, and together they challenged the might of Rome. When their combined armies were defeated by Octavius in 30 CE, Cleopatra committed suicide. From then on, Egypt became a mere Roman province, ruled over by the emperors.

TIME-HONORED TRADITION

Two of the principal roles for women were to make and wash the clothes for the family. The most common material was linen, woven from the stems of the flax plant, making a strong and durable fabric. The first loom appeared in Egypt around 3000 BCE.

QUEEN NEFERTITI

Women rarely ruled in their own right in ancient Egypt, although there are a few notable exceptions. Queen Nefertiti, who ruled with her husband Akhenaten, was much hated and after their deaths both their names were removed from many books and inscriptions. She aided Akhenaten in banishing the worship of all the old gods, including Amun-Re, in favor of Aten, a sun god. Around 1333 BCE, Tutankhamen restored the old gods to prominence.

HARVESTING

Much of the agricultural work was performed by women and children. The woman shown here is picking fruit whilst carrying her child in a kind of papoose.

GALLEYS

Egyptian war galleys usually took the form of huge barges, used simply to transport men and supplies. They were sometimes fitted with a massive battering ram at the bow to sink enemy ships.

FINE BLADES

Egyptian battles usually followed the same basic plan. First, archers (often mounted on chariots) rained arrows upon the enemy, followed by spearsmen who pushed them back. The final stage, when the enemy was in disarray, was to send in swordsmen, using either daggers or short swords. They were used as stabbing weapons rather than for striking, so the blades were often made of copper which, although softer than bronze, kept a better edge. The beautifully engraved daggers shown here came from Tutankhamen's tomb.

CHARIOTS

Sometime around 3000 BCE, the Sumerians first attached wheels to carts (formerly pulled on sled-like arrangements). Soon after, war chariots were invented. They were small two-wheeled vehicles, pulled by horses, which carried two men, a driver and a soldier. There were no seats, simply a platform from which the soldier attacked an enemy with bow or spear while the driver charged the enemy lines. Egypt quickly followed Sumer's lead and adopted war chariots, giving them a military edge over their enemies.

War & Weaponry

From about 5000-3100 BCE two separate kingdoms flourished; Upper and Lower Egypt. In about 3100 BCE, King Menes united the two kingdoms and founded the I dynasty. Egyptian civilization flourished after that date, but settlements were mostly centered in the Nile valley itself. During what is known as the New Kingdom period (*c.*1550-1070 BCE), Egypt expanded its domains to form a small empire, stretching from Nubia in the south, to Sumer and Syria in the north. Although generally not a war-like nation, in order to protect its borders Egypt adopted an aggressive stance towards its neighbors. Egypt was a rich country and often attracted the greedy attentions of other nations, so much of the efforts of its army were concentrated on protecting itself. Later Egypt was subjected to wave after wave of invasion, when the greatness of their earlier civilization fell. It then became a mere province of first the Persians, followed by the Greeks, Romans and Arabs, who supplanted Egyptian culture with their own.

TACTICS

The army was a highly organized and well-disciplined fighting machine. The usual tactics were for the soldiers to march in divisions of about 50 straight towards the enemy lines and overcome them by sheer weight of numbers. The pharaoh usually participated in military campaigns. Ramesses II is seen here overcoming his enemies, the Nubians, Libyans and Syrians.

WARRIORS

The favored weapons in the Egyptian army were the spear and the battle-axe. Axes were often quite elaborate, with bronze heads. Soldiers had comparatively light armor, usually helmets and large wooden shields, used as protection against arrows or the thrusting spear of an enemy soldier.

PROTECTION OF THE GODS

When the Egyptians undertook a military campaign, they invoked the power of the gods to both protect and assist them in striking down their enemies. Wars were fought with great pomp and ceremony, with trumpeters to accompany the army. A mast was carried on the pharaoh's chariot, decorated with a ram's head and a symbol of the sun to represent Amun-Re. Many other gods might accompany the army, including Khansu the moon god, shown here.

Crime & Punishment

Egyptian society demanded strict codes of law that everyone was expected to follow. By modern standards, some of these laws might seem harsh, but most pharaohs worked on the assumption that if the citizens were properly protected against crime then they would not only be more content but would give more back to society itself. Some laws were introduced to promote better hygiene, such as compulsory circumcision. It was everyone's duty to prevent or report crimes, or to go to someone's aid if they were in danger. To not do so was in itself a crime. Crimes against women were punished by mutilation: adulterous women were made ugly by having their noses amputated, whilst pregnant women who had committed a crime were only punished after they had given birth. Similarly, forgers had their hands cut off and those guilty of treason had their tongues removed. A soldier guilty of any crime had to make amends by performing a heroic deed.

COUNTERFEIT

A coined monetary system was not introduced into Egypt until 525 BCE when the Persians invaded. After that date anyone found guilty of making counterfeit coins had their hands cut off. The gold coin shown here is of Cleopatra's time (c. 40 CE).

ALL-SEEING GOD

The pharaoh was thought to be the embodiment of the hawk-headed sky god Horus. He was an all-seeing god who ensured that every citizen was protected. If a guilty person escaped accusation and punishment in life, they might still pay the price in death. If they were justly accused of a crime, even after death, they might be denied burial honors and so be robbed of the opportunity to enter the afterlife.

SLAVE TRADE

This relief from the temple of Ramesses III shows defeated Philistines being led into captivity with a rope tied around their necks. Egyptian society made great use of slaves captured from defeated countries, particularly in the years of the New Kingdom, after 1550 BCE. Slaves provided much of the labor for the massive building programmes of the pharaohs and many died in the process.

CITIZEN'S DUTY

Egyptian society was largely self-policing. It was the duty of every citizen to prevent crimes or to follow up with their punishment. Everyone had the right to accuse and prosecute a criminal. If witnesses did not fulfil their duty they were beaten with branches.

LAW OF DECLARATION

Each year every individual had to provide a written report to the magistrate of the province in which they lived stating how they made their legal means of existence, whether as bakers as shown above, herdsmen or scribes. If they did not, it was assumed they did so illegally and were executed.

HONOR AMONG THIEVES

mong other things, Thoth was the god of wisdom and truth. He had the ability to know the evils that lay in men's hearts and is seen here, in baboon form, apprehending a thief. Strangely, thieves could register their profession and declare their earnings to an official, but if a victim of theft could accurately describe his possessions, he could claim 75% of his goods back; the remaining 25% remained the property of the thief.

Transport & Science

The ancient Egyptians were responsible for introducing or developing many new ideas. Several, such as the potter's wheel, are still in use today. Although it is now believed that Egypt (and indeed the whole of north Africa) was less arid than it is today, natural materials such as wood were never in abundance. However, stone and papyrus were, and the Egyptians were very resourceful in making maximum use of these commodities. Papyrus is a triangular-stemmed reed that grows to a height of about 13 feet (3 meters). All parts of the plant were used, and so extensively that it almost disappeared completely, although it has now been re-introduced into Egypt. As most of the main centers of population were scattered down the length of the Nile, most long-distance journeys were made by boat. Egyptian boats were not particularly seaworthy and were used mostly on the calmer waters of the Nile itself.

PALANQUIN

The pharoah and other important dignitaries were transported in a chariot or a decorated carriage for long journeys. For short journeys around the city, they would be carried in a palanquin, which was a canopied chair carried on two poles by four servants.

TIME IMMEMORIAL

Egyptian priests were also astronomers. By studying the movements of heavenly bodies they were able to accurately predict various natural phenomena, which they used in religious ceremonies. They devised an annual calendar of 365 days, divided into 12 equal months of 30 days, followed by five "complementary" days.

WHEELED VEHICLES

About 3000 BCE the Sumerians are believed to have created the first wheeled vehicle. The idea was soon copied and developed by the Egyptians, who made many more sophisticated vehicles, though none survive.

THE SKY GOD

The Egyptians studied the heavens in great detail and formed a fairly acceptable theory as to the origins of the universe. They saw the primeval chaos of the universe as water (Nun). The sun god Amun-Re emerged from the sea as land (as Egypt itself did from the annual flood). From this were produced air (Shu), moisture (Tefnut), earth (Geb) and sky (Nut). Nut visited her earth husband daily by descending from the heavens and creating night. Eclipses were explained by Nut supposedly stealing away to visit Geb during the day.

REED BOATS

Many of the boats used in ancient Egypt were not made of wood, which was expensive and difficult to obtain, but of the much more readily available papyrus. The reeds were tightly bundled and then strapped to a frame, in a similar manner to roof thatching. They were made waterproof by lashing several layers together, which could be easily replaced if they became rotten or damaged. Propelled by oars, most fishermen used this kind of vessel.

WRITING IT ALL DOWN

Flat strips of papyrus were used in layers to form a very smooth and durable paper, usually cut into lengths and rolled into scrolls. Even the pens used to write with were made from papyrus stems.

RIVER TRANSPORT

This model, found in a tomb, is probably typical of many of the boats that plied the Nile. It was propelled by oars and a small sail and steered with a large oar at the stern, like a rudder.

THOTH

According to the sacred writings of ancient Egypt, Thoth was the divine intelligence of the universe, credited with teaching man articulate language, writing, art, music, architecture, mathematics, and name-giving. He was the god of the moon and is often represented by the ibis, whose curved beak resembles the crescent moon.

ANUBIS

Anubis, the god of mummification, was represented by a jackal. Jackals frequented cemeteries (probably to eat corpses) but they were seen as protectors of the dead. The priest shown here is wearing a jackal mask and is opening the mouth of the deceased during the mummification process to restore the use of the senses, and thus restoring life in the next world.

THE SPHINX

Standing within the extraordinary complex of monuments at Giza is a sphinx; half-man, half-lion. Carved from the solid rock in about 2500 BC it is some 117 feet (35.6 meters) long and 51 feet (15.5 meters) high. Originally the head was lavishly decorated. Its purpose remains a mystery, but may have been intended to guard the pharaoh's tomb.

CULT OF THE DEAD

To the ancient Egyptians, death was seen simply as a temporary phase between this life and the afterlife. Bodies of the deceased were preserved by mummification and spells were written on coffins. Books of the Dead were buried with the bodies (detail shown right), from which the deceased were to recite to ensure safe passage to the next life.

Religion

There were several hundred different gods and goddesses in ancient Egypt, many of whom manifested themselves as animals on earth. When priests carried out their rituals they would often wear the appropriate animal mask so as to give the impression to the largely uneducated masses that they were the actual god. It is not easy to unravel the complexities of the Egyptian gods, especially as the same animal might represent several different gods in different regions. However, the one "true god," and king of all the other gods, was Amun-Re, the sun god. The ancient Egyptians kept many libraries of books, mostly of sacred writings, and many talk of a belief in an afterlife. They believed in an underworld, called Duat, where the dead had to make a perilous journey to reach a kind of "promised land." To aid them in their journey, bodies were mummified (or preserved) and they were given magic spells to ward off the evils they would encounter.

THE TEMPLE OF KARNAK

The magnificent temple at Karnak was begun between 1504-1592 BCE. The columns and walls are decorated with lotus and papyrus carvings, two of the most enduring ancient Egyptian symbols. The temple, like many others, was dedicated to Amun-Re, protector of the pharaohs. Amun-Re is an amalgam of Amun (which means "hidden") and Re (the sun god). He was perceived as the "great primordial being"; the "one true god."

THE SACRED TRIAD

Amun-Re was perceived as a triad of divinities, Amun (the father), Mouth (the mother) and Khons (the son). They manifested themselves on earth as Osiris, Isis and Horus, respectively.

ISIS

This picture shows the goddess Isis, suckling her infant son, Horus. Isis and Osiris were instructed by Thoth to civilize the human race and lead them away from the ways of animals. Isis was a fertility goddess, associated with mother Earth and the cycle of birth, death and re-birth in the afterlife. Her shrines in temples were often tended by women. The Romans adopted her into their own religion following their conquest of Egypt.

Legacy of the Past

Incredibly, the pyramid complex at Giza (main picture), which includes the Great Pyramid of Khufu, is only a short distance from modern-day Cairo, a lasting testament to one of the greatest civilizations of the ancient world. Although not the oldest civilization known (though it was once thought to be) it has left a lasting impression, certainly in the monumental legacy of its architecture. The ancient Greeks were directly influenced by what they found there, which greatly influenced the development of their civilization and, in turn, that of the Romans. It is also believed that the Egyptians first devised the unit of time known as a "week," naming the seven days after each of the five known planets (Mars, Mercury, Jupiter, Venus and Saturn), the sun and the moon.

TUTANKHAMEN'S TREASURE

King Tutankhamen lived during the XVIII dynasty and died at the age of 18 in *c.*1344 BCE. When his tomb was opened in 1922, it was the only tomb of a pharaoh, so far discovered, to survive intact. Inside was an astonishing array of jewelry, artefacts and decorative art, unsurpassed in the ancient world. His magnificent funerary face mask, shown above, was made of gold, inlaid with blue lapis lazuli.

Treasures from the tomb have been displayed around the world and always generate a great deal of interest. The exhibition in Cairo Museum is now a major tourist attraction in its own right.

WRITTEN IN THE STARS

It was the astronomer priests of ancient Egypt who, around 2500 BCE, first devised the zodiac, still in use today. In those days astrology and astronomy were seen as the same thing and given a great deal of scientific credibility. By observing the heavens over many centuries and carefully recording their findings, Egyptian astronomers divided the skies into 12 constellations, each closely representing a particular aspect of their beliefs.

architrave *capital*

UNIQUE ARCHITECTURE

Egyptian architecture displays many characteristics that are unique and set it apart from European styles of building. The closest parallels are to be seen in the Aztec and Inca buildings of South and Central America (coincidentally, also pyramid builders of a later age). The most striking features are the irregularly shaped and incredibly accurate masonry joints, and the columns, which have square blocks on top of the capitals to support the architrave above.

THE POTTER'S WHEEL

Of all the technological achievements handed down to us by the ancient Egyptians, perhaps the most enduring is the potter's wheel. Invented around 4000 BCE it changed the face of civilization for all time, enabling elaborate pieces to be mass-produced for the first time. Operated by a simple treadle mechanism, the basic design has hardly changed at all.

Who were the Ancient Greeks?

ncient Greece is regarded by many as the cradle of civilization in Europe but unlike Rome and other civilizations that followed, it did not consist of one centrally controlled empire. Early Greek civilizations were greatly influenced by nearby Egypt and Sumeria. The first of these was the Minoan, centered on the island of Crete, which flourished between *c.*2000-1400 BCE. On the Greek mainland, the dominant civilization was the Mycenaean, *c.*1600-1100 BCE. After that, Greece entered a "Dark Age," of which very little is known, until the emergence in the 8th century BCE of a number of independent city-states. Each one forged links with, and was influenced by the others. They in turn rose to power, usually by invasion rather than by agreement. As each did so, new sites were chosen for their cities, which has resulted in many sites lying undisturbed over the centuries, albeit in ruins as locals frequently raided them for building materials. The result of this pattern of development has enabled historians and archeologists to peel back these various layers of civilization and view them in isolation.

PULLING TOGETHER

Although the Greek city-states acted independently, one of the rare times they worked together was in the Trojan Wars *c.*1184 BCE. The Mycenaean king, Agamemnon, united the Greeks against Troy, defeating them with the use of a huge wooden horse.

GREEK TOWNS

The center of every Greek town followed very much the same plan. Built on hills for defense, the civic and religious buildings were close together as they were central to Greek society.

THE TEMPLE

The main temple usually occupied the highest point of the acropolis and was intended to impress both the people and the gods.

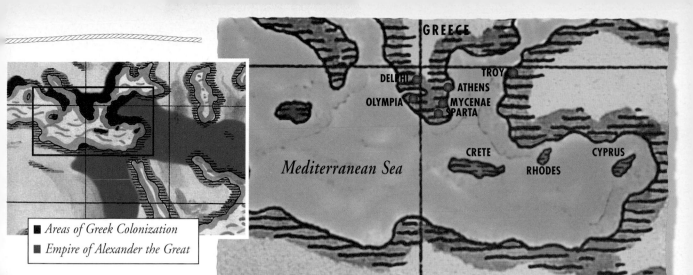

Areas of Greek Colonization
Empire of Alexander the Great

GREECE

DELPHI
OLYMPIA
ATHENS
MYCENAE
SPARTA
TROY

Mediterranean Sea

CRETE
RHODES
CYPRUS

SPIRITUAL CENTER

The Omphalos Stone (shown here) was thought to mark the center of the universe. According to myth, Zeus wanted to measure the world so he set two eagles free from opposite ends of the Earth. They met over Delphi so Zeus decreed that this was the world's center, and the site assumed profound religious importance.

THE FIRST EUROPEANS

The earliest known civilization in Europe flourished on Crete in the eastern Mediterranean. It was named Minoan, after the legendary King Minos who was said to rule the Aegean sea. Excavations of the palace of Knossos in northern Crete have revealed that its inhabitants enjoyed a sophisticated lifestyle. It was highly decorated and had an advanced drainage and water-supply system.

THE AMPHITHEATER

Every major town had an open-air theater, called an amphitheater.

THE ACROPOLIS

At the highest point of the town was a citadel or walled enclosure. This housed the most important town buildings; the temples and government buildings.

THE AGORA

In the center was the *agora*, a large open space where people met and conducted business.

THE COLOSSUS OF RHODES

Once part of Macedonia, in *c.*408 BCE the islanders of Rhodes formed themselves into an independent state. The island was unsuccessfully besieged by Demetrios in 305-304 BCE, following the removal of a Macedonian garrison by the Rhodians. To mark their victory they built the Colossus, a gigantic statue of the sun god, Helios. It stood 101 feet (31 meters) high and straddled the harbor entrance. One of the "Seven Wonders of the World," it was destroyed by an earthquake in *c.*227 BCE.

FINE CRAFTSMANSHIP

As food was easily available at the town's market, not everyone needed to grow their own. Workers could develop other skills to trade and the Greek potters became fine craftsmen.

Using local clay, they produced beautifully decorated items including plates, dishes, wine goblets, bottles and vases for both the home market and for export. Many of these items have survived intact, and the intricate designs tell us much about the Greek lifestyle.

ELEGANT CLOTHES

This carved relief from a temple shows the typical clothes worn by the wealthier Greeks. Whereas the poor had to rely on home-spun linen or woollen clothes, the rich could afford to buy exotic imported materials, such as fine cotton and silk from India and the East. The rich employed the services of tailors or bought ready-made clothes from merchants. Both sexes wore a *chitan* made from two large pieces of rectangular material fastened at the sides and neck, but worn loose, like a tunic. Women wore their clothes to ankle length; men to the knee.

SLAVE TRADE

Like most ancient civilizations, Greece relied heavily on slave labour. Slavery served two main purposes: it showed the superiority of the victorious Greeks over the peoples of conquered lands, and big money was made by selling slaves to wealthy Greeks as servants and cheap labor.

Life for the Rich

The rich mostly lived in large town houses, conveniently close to all the town's facilities. The very rich might also have had a house in the country. Despite the often grand designs of Greek civic buildings and temples, homes were not particularly ornate— the rich just had larger houses with more rooms than those of the poor. Most wealthy men were engaged in government or commerce, so it was essential to live in towns in order to conduct their business. For the wives of wealthy men, the house was virtually a prison. Slaves carried out the mundane domestic duties that usually brought women into contact with others, so few ventured out without their husbands.

SIMPLE TASTES

Houses, even for the rich, were basic, made from dried mud bricks (painted white to deflect the heat of the sun) or stone. They had tiled roofs, stone floors and a small open courtyard, perhaps containing a private well. Windows were few, to keep the interior cool and shady. The rooms were simply but comfortably furnished, as this vase illustration shows. Their beds had mattresses, pillows and bedding, and other furniture included tables and footstools.

DEATH MASK

This beautiful mask of beaten gold was believed to be the funerary mask of Agamemnon, the legendary king of Mycenae who died in the 12th century BCE. In fact, it is probably much older than that, possibly 500 years older. Such masks were commonly used in royal burials and show the wealth of the Mycenaean civilization at the time.

RAISE YOUR GLASS

The technique of glass-blowing was not perfected until Roman times. Prior to that, glass was an expensive commodity and difficult to work. Most drinking vessels were made of clay, therefore, but the rich would buy goblets made of glass to show their wealth and impress their friends.

Life for the Poor

Although most of the remains from ancient Greece are grand, in terms of both scale and design, this gives a rather misguided view of their society. A fortunate few were wealthy and enjoyed a luxurious lifestyle, but most of the population were poor, carving their living from the land as best they could. The barren Greek soils and dry climate often gave poor harvests, and peasants were sometimes forced to leave the poorer regions and help populate the new colonies in the empire rather than face starvation. However hard-working, people of all classes took their leisure time seriously. Many religious festivals coincided with the bringing in of the harvest, when everyone in the village joined in and celebrated the season's crop.

EARTHENWARE

Pottery for the poorer classes was much simpler, less decorative and more functional than for the rich. Life was a struggle for existence and there was little time or money to expend on unnecessary luxuries. Plates, pots and drinking vessels were usually made from unglazed clay, molded by hand and left to dry in the sun.

BEASTS OF BURDEN

The most common beast of burden was the donkey or mule. They are very sure-footed animals which was particularly important in the mountainous and rocky terrain of Greece. Peasant farmers often used their donkeys to travel considerable distances from villages to reach their fields. Donkeys were also used as pack animals, as they still are today in the poorer regions of Greece, to take produce to market in the towns. For the very poor who could not afford an ox, donkeys were even used to pull the plow.

ALL PULL TOGETHER

The Greeks did not operate a centrally organized system of agriculture. Each farmer grew his own food and had his own oxen to pull the plow. Poorer communities would sometimes share a team of oxen, with each family taking its turn. In order to help feed the growing population, it was necessary for the Greeks to expand their empire. They set up colonies around the Mediterranean to enable Greek merchants to import any shortfall in food supply. They would trade luxury goods in exchange for grain.

SIMPLE HOMES

For the poor, houses were simple, with few concessions to luxury. They were built from dried mud bricks, plastered with wet mud and painted white to deflect the summer heat. Window openings were few and unglazed and roofs were either thatched or tiled. The construction and style was not hugely different from houses and churches still seen in Greece today. They would have had only one main room where the entire family lived and ate. Communal bedrooms occupied a loft-like upper floor and furnishings were few, usually comprising of just a table, chairs and beds.

SUBSISTENCE FARMING

The majority of the population lived in remote villages, scattered throughout the land and often separated from one another by the mountains. Peasants eked out a subsistence form of farming, each growing just enough to feed their own family. Fortunately, most communities were located close to the sea so the poor could supplement their diet with fresh seafood. Any surplus of food was taken to market to trade for other commodities, such as shoes and wine. Most families, including the poorer townsfolk, would also keep a few goats for milk and cheese and chickens for eggs.

LEISURE TIME

One of the most popular pastimes in ancient Greece was attending plays, pageants or festivals at the town's amphitheater. Performances were free or inexpensive, subsidised by rich benefactors or politicians who wished to win favor with the populace, and so even the poor could enjoy the festivities. Women were not encouraged to attend, though they were probably not actually banned from doing so, but they were certainly excluded from taking part in the performances. To become an actor was one of the few means of escape from the drudgery of poverty for boys.

SEAFOOD

The Mediterranean Sea is abundant with seafood, particularly
octopus and squid, which still forms an important part of Greek cuisine today.
The usual method of cooking was to cut the tentacles into small slices and to boil or fry
them in olive oil. Common fish still caught in Greek waters are tuna, mullet, and mackerel.

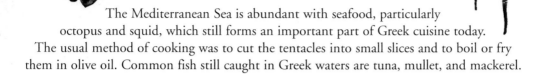

OLIVE GROVES

The goddess Athena supposedly introduced the olive tree into Greece.
Olives were either eaten or pressed to make oil, used in cooking,
rubbed into the skin, or burnt for lighting. Olive trees grow
profusely in Greece and still provide a valuable source of
income for farmers today.

VINTAGE WINE

The most common drink for Greeks of all
classes was wine. Sometimes this was drunk
undiluted, but usually water was added
because of the vast quantities consumed.
The wine was quite thick and did not
keep well; it was usually
strained before drinking.
The Greeks knew the
importance of a clean
water supply, and
sometimes wine was
also used as a means
of purifying water.

HOME COOKING

This terracotta figure from Crete, made
in the 6th century BCE, shows a woman
stirring food in a saucepan with a
ladle. She may be making stew, or
perhaps porridge. Vegetables were
often made into a stew and eaten with
bread, but the Greeks also enjoyed
salads dressed with garlic and olive oil.
Cooking was often done outdoors, to
avoid smells and the risk of fire. Inside, meals
were cooked on stone hearths using charcoal to
grill the food. Clay ovens were used for baking.

Food & Drink

As in most societies, ancient and modern, the wealthy Greeks ate very well, enjoying a wide variety of foods, while the poor had to make do with a more limited diet. However, all Greeks knew the importance of good food to their health, and they had a balanced diet consisting of protein, fiber, vegetables, and dairy produce. Most people in rural areas grew their own food and tended their own animals. Even in towns many households kept a goat for fresh milk and cheese, and perhaps a few chickens for eggs. Meat was not widely eaten by the poor, except perhaps at religious festivals, but the rich enjoyed a variety of meats, including boar, deer, and rabbit. Fortunately the waters of the Mediterranean provided a bountiful supply of seafood for everyone. Wine and water were the most common drinks. Fruit juices, such as fig juice, or honey were used to sweeten food. Herbs and spices from the East were used to garnish vegetables and salads, or to disguise the often rancid taste of rotten food.

SOURCE OF PROTEIN

As many settlements were sited near the coast, the sea provided a plentiful supply of alternative protein to meat, which the poor could not afford.

DAILY BREAD

The staple diet for many Greeks was bread made with wheat or barley flour. Greek bread was quite coarse and stodgy and was baked in flat, round loaves. A great favorite at breakfast-time was to soak bread in olive oil or wine, and eat it with figs or other fruit. The decorative loaf shown here was probably made for a banquet.

MUSIC AND DANCE

Music and dancing were popular with Greeks from all classes, not only as a pastime but also at religious festivals. Musicians often accompanied plays at the theater or performed at private banquets. Common musical instruments of the time included flutes, pan-pipes, harps, and lyres.

THEATER-GOING

Most Greek cities had an amphitheater at their center. This was an open-air theater where plays or enactments of stories of the gods and legendary heroes were popular. The plays were usually comedies or tragedies, and all the actors wore a mask to depict their character. Simple scene changes also added an air of mystery to the entertainment. All actors were men, with boys playing the women's roles.

LEGENDARY HEROES

One of the principal pastimes in the home was storytelling. Children would gather round to hear their parents recount legendary tales of past Greek heroes, or of the exploits of the gods. One such story is of Theseus slaying the Minotaur, a hybrid monster, half-bull, half-man, kept by the legendary King Minos in a labyrinth at Knossos, Crete.

DISCUS THROWING

Statues depicting discus throwing seem to have been popular, and perhaps these athletes represent the spirit of the Olympic Games more than any other. Like other events, discus throwing has its origins in warfare, as a means of training soldiers to hurl objects with accuracy at an enemy. The discus was generally larger and heavier than those used today, and was made of stone or bronze.

THE OLYMPIC GAMES

The most important sporting event in ancient Greece was the Olympic Games, first established in 776 BCE. Held on a rota basis every four years, the games were staged in Olympia and were conceived as a means of honoring the gods. Inevitably they became an outward show of the rivalry between the various city-states. Athletes traveled from far and wide to compete. Winning athletes brought honor to their home state and enjoyed celebrity status. In 1896 the ideal of the Olympic Games was revived and the first modern games were held in this stadium in Athens.

Pastimes

We know a great deal about how the ancient Greeks spent their leisure time because of the abundance of surviving art and artefacts depicting scenes of everyday life. Greek culture was based on a slave society, with captured slaves from newly-conquered lands performing many of the menial tasks. This left many Greeks, particularly the rich, with plenty of time on their hands. Leisure was seen as an essential part of everyday life, especially sporting activities which were regarded as necessary for good health. Sports also provided an important method of training for warfare and as a means of honoring the gods. Music, dancing and theater-going were other popular pastimes, as were board games, gambling and horse and chariot racing.

THE JAVELIN THROWER

This stone relief depicts a Greek javelin thrower. Javelins were long, light spears specially balanced for throwing, and were originally made as a form of weapon training. It became one of the most popular events at sporting games.

Fashion

Greeks of all classes were very conscious of their appearance and spent a great deal of their time and money on their hairstyles, clothes and jewelry. The rivalry between the various city-states even extended to fashion—the people of one state believing themselves more sophisticated than the others.

Clothes were often white or brightly colored. For the poorer classes, finely-spun woollen textiles were common, while the rich displayed their wealth by importing exotic fabrics from the Far East, such as silk and cotton. The Greeks seemed quite unselfconscious about their bodies. Athletes, both male and female, usually performed naked, and women's clothing was often made of light, transparent materials which, although cool to wear, could also be quite revealing.

ELABORATE HAIRSTYLES

Women used decorative pins and slides to hold their hair in place, while for men it was fashionable to curl their hair, as shown here.

NOVELTY VALUE

This beautiful perfume pot, made of decorated clay with a wax stopper, was probably made in either Corinth or Rhodes. Both regions were renowned for producing unusual novelty ware, such as this, for export. Greeks were quite fastidious about their personal hygiene and both men and women wore perfume.

PROPER DRESS

We know a great deal about the clothes worn by ordinary men and women from the beautiful decorations on Greek pottery, such as on this vase. Clothes for both sexes were quite similar, consisting of simple tunics, fastened at the shoulder by a brooch. Women tended to wear their clothes longer as it was considered improper to wear them short.

AN AGE OF ELEGANCE

Jewelry was popular amongst all classes and was often an indication of a person's wealth. Poorer people wore jewelry made of cheaper materials, such as bronze or ceramics. The rich preferred to use jewelry made of gold or silver. Although precious and semi-precious stones were used, Greek jewelers preferred to use delicately crafted gold and silver pendants and chains, fashioned into intricate designs. The replica earring shown here came from Troy (the original was dated *c.*2300 BCE). It was usual for the Greeks to have pierced ears.

REFLECTED BEAUTY

Many people might be surprised at the degree of sophistication enjoyed in Greek society, certainly at the higher levels. Many of the everyday items still currently in use, and which we might regard as modern, had their counterparts in the ancient world, like this bronze mirror. The carving on its stand is the goddess Aphrodite, the goddess of love and beauty. The rear panel was beautifully engraved while the front would have been highly polished to show a reflection. As we do today, most Greeks adorned themselves with make-up and jewelry.

SKIN DEEP

Beauty and personal hygiene were considered very important to the Greeks. Physical exercise and caring for the body was seen as essential to good health. It was fashionable to wash regularly, not in large communal baths, like the Romans, but in small tubs in the privacy of their own houses. They anointed their bodies with olive oil to ensure a good complexion. Both men and women wore perfumes and used cosmetics to color the skin as a sun tan was considered unattractive. Most people wore hats (like bonnets) as protection from the sun and wore simple, leather sandals on their feet, as worn by this girl on a typical vase decoration.

Art & Architecture

The art and architecture of the ancient Greeks has perhaps been the most influential of any other civilization. They developed a style of architecture, based upon Egyptian examples, using tall columns supporting heavy lintels to create large, grand civic buildings that still inspire architects today. State and religious buildings were decorated with statues and stone friezes, displaying great skills in stone masonry. They were equally skilful as artists, as can be seen by surviving wall paintings, and the most popular medium— the splendid pottery produced at the time. Artists created scenes from the stories of Greek mythology, or depicted everyday Greek life.

THE POTTER'S ART

Pottery, as well as being appreciated for its artistic value, can also be used to date the society that created it. Greek pottery was mostly made from locally excavated clay, made on a wheel and fired in ovens. It can be roughly dated according to its design. Up to about 700 BCE geometric patterns were popular. This was replaced by a fashion for oriental designs and black-figures until approximately 500 BCE when the red-figure technique took over.

WALL PAINTINGS

The walls of many Greek buildings were adorned with fine frescoes and paintings. The wall painting shown here, depicting dolphins and fish, is a restoration and comes from the Queen's Room in the Palace of Knossos, Crete (*c.*1500 BCE).

ARCHITECTURAL STYLES

The dominant features of Greek buildings were the rows of columns supporting the roof beams (lintels). The tops of the columns (capitals) were highly decorated. The three main styles were plain (known as Doric), scroll-topped (Ionic, as shown) or highly decorated with leaf and other designs (Corinthian).

THE ACROPOLIS

The acropolis was the upper fortified section of all Greek cities. This main picture shows the Acropolis in Athens, dominated by the temple of the Parthenon (which means "virgin"), built between 447 and 432 BCE.

Health & Medicine

The Greeks inherited their interest in the study of medicine from the Egyptians, whom they greatly admired. Unlike the Egyptians however, whose physicians specialized in specific areas of the body and treated them in isolation, Greek doctors tended to regard the function of each part in relation to the whole body to promote general good health. They also believed in adopting a good bedside manner and administering a daily dose of wine. Operations to remove infected parts were carried out, but usually only as a last resort. Like so much else in Greek life, health and medicine were dominated by religion. Prayers and offerings were made to the gods, particularly Asclepios. If a patient was cured, they would often leave a model or other token depicting the affected part of the body, as an offering to the gods. It is not known what the average life expectancy was, but certainly the wealthier citizens lived to ages in excess of 70.

THE GOD OF MEDICINE

Asclepios, a son of Apollo, was the god of medicine and healing. Ancient Greeks believed that illness and disease were sent by the gods as a punishment if they were offended. Temples dedicated to Asclepios were amongst the most common in the Greek world, with a special caste of priests practicing medicine in his name. In many pagan religions, the serpent (as seen here entwined round his staff) is seen as the "life-force" flowing through all things and is held sacred.

HEALTHY LIFESTYLES

Sick people traveled many miles to seek cures at the shrines of Asclepios, where the priests prescribed various herbal cures and special diets. One of the principle forms of preventative medicine was exercise, to both appease the gods and generate healthy well-being. Boys were encouraged to practice athletics as training for the army and girls to promote healthy child-bearing.

FOUNDER OF MODERN MEDICINE

Hippocrates (460-377 BCE) was a distinguished physician, who was born and studied medicine on the island of Kos. He started teaching in the open, under a plane tree (shown left)—one still grows on the island in commemoration of him. Hippocrates wrote 53 medical books, known as "the Corpus." He believed that the human body was a single organism and the individual parts should not be treated separately. He established a code of medical ethics, which doctors still subscribe to today (the Hippocratic Oath).

PERSONAL HYGIENE

The Greeks recognized the importance of personal cleanliness and hygiene to maintain good health. They did not partake in hot and cold plunge baths like the Romans, but did wash frequently in private tubs in their homes. They also used olive oil to deep-cleanse the skin.

SANITATION

From a very early date the Greeks constructed sophisticated water supply and drainage systems. The two systems were kept separate to prevent the spread of disease. Fine examples are to be seen in the palaces and towns of Crete (c.2000 BCE) such as Malia and Knossos. Clay pipes buried in the walls distributed clean water from vast reservoirs, while underground channels cut into the stone carried away the waste water.

Love & Marriage

Most marriages in ancient Greece were arranged between both sets of parents. Usually a father would select a husband (often much older) for his daughter when she reached the age of 12 or 13. When courting, a young man would pay a great deal of attention to his intended bride, but once married it was a different story. Wives were considered the property of their husbands and were expected to obey him. Married women were jealously guarded by their husbands, and were seldom allowed to meet or talk to other men unless he was present. In Sparta, men were not allowed to marry until the age of 20. The groom had to pretend to carry his bride off, caveman fashion. To test his courage and initiative, the newly-wed Spartan was kept apart from his wife for some time and only allowed to visit her by stealth. If caught, he was punished.

GODDESS OF LOVE

Aphrodite was the Greek goddess of love and beauty. She is nearly always shown as a beautiful young woman, either naked or semi-clothed. On the day of their wedding, brides made offerings to her shrine to ensure a happy marriage.

SPARTAN GIRLS

These young girls come from Sparta, a powerful Greek state that at one time rivaled the power of Athens. In Sparta, the emphasis was on the collective well-being of the state. Both young men and women were encouraged to compete in athletics in order to produce a "super-race" of soldiers, and so the girls would bear healthy babies. As a result of being treated more as equals, Spartan girls seemed more promiscuous, by comparison, than girls from other states.

VIRTUOUS WIVES

The main purpose in marriage for both a man and a woman was to give birth to sons to carry on the family line. Conversely to the norm, in much of Greece the more wealthy and important a man was, the more restricted his wife was likely to be. She would have been confined to an area of the house called the Women's Quarter. This enabled the man to entertain without the fear of the other guests meeting his wife—whose virtue was paramount. Domestic duties were given to the servants, so rich wives rarely ventured out of the house.

UNREQUITED LOVE

The theme of unrequited love is a common one in Greek mythology, amongst both mortals and the gods. The illustration shown here depicts the sun god, Apollo, and Daphne, a nymph and daughter of the river god, Perseus. Apollo pursued Daphne, but she resisted his advances and asked for help from the king of the gods, Zeus, by praying to him. In answer to her prayers, Zeus turned her into a laurel tree, which afterwards became sacred to Apollo and he often wore a laurel wreath on his head in memory of his lost love. Greek brides often wear laurel wreaths in their hair during the marriage ceremony.

NYMPHS

Nymphs were not gods, but semi-divine female spirits, often associated with nature and fertility. In general, the Greeks had a fairly liberal attitude towards sex and nudity, as can be seen in the immodest poses in much of their art and statuary. Women on the island of Lesbos seem to have enjoyed greater freedom than women in other states. They were, for example, allowed a say in choosing their partners and to express themselves in art.

Women & Children

Women in Greek society were very much regarded as second-class citizens and enjoyed few rights. Attitudes varied between the various city-states, but by and large women were held in low regard. Few women were allowed to hold positions of authority and if a woman had money or property these automatically passed to her husband on marriage. Poorer women, unusually, enjoyed more freedom than their rich counterparts, for they at least were allowed to work or meet with friends in the market place. Only sons were treated with any degree of reverence; girls were married off as soon as possible and received no education. There were no schools, as such. The wealthy would pay for private tutors for their sons.

PUT AWAY YOUR CHILDISH THINGS

On reaching the age of 12 children were considered young adults. Boys dedicated their toys to Apollo, girls to his twin sister, Artemis, as a sign of their maturity. Artemis was goddess of the hunt and her shrines were often attended by women.

HELEN OF TROY

Women in ancient Greece were regarded as male possessions, so when Helen (supposedly the most beautiful woman in Greece, and wife of the Spartan king Menelaus) was taken by Paris to Troy, it was considered such a slight that it was one of the rare times that the Greeks became a united army. According to mythology, the Greeks besieged Troy for 10 years to rescue her and the story became the basis for Homer's epic poem, *The Iliad*.

HELD IN THE BALANCE

Greek fathers had the right to decide whether a new-born baby lived or died. If the child was sickly, or if it was a girl, they had the right to abandon the baby if they could not afford to keep it. Such babies were left in the open air to die, though some might be saved by childless families and adopted. Others were rescued, only to become slaves. Those children who survived this harsh judgement were usually well cared for.

LEARNING BY ROTE

At age 7, boys from rich families began their education. The usual subjects were reading, writing, math, poetry and music, learnt by reciting out loud. On rare occasions, the daughters of rich families received private tuition. Some tutors would travel between towns and would conduct lessons in the open air. Children from poor families received no education at all.

CHILDREN AT PLAY

A typical Greek childhood was comparatively short. By the age of 12, boys were often undergoing physical training for the army and girls might already be married. Those children who remained at home after then were expected to help support the family. Children played with a variety of toys, including dolls, soldiers and board games. Greek families were quite large, but child mortality was also quite high. Only about half of those born could expect to reach age 20.

KOUROS

This marble statue of a naked young boy is called a "kouros." They were placed in shrines dedicated to Apollo, god of light and healing. There is some evidence to suggest that children were used in certain religious rituals, their innocence symbolizing virtue.

A WOMAN'S LOT

A woman's lot in ancient Greece was certainly not a happy one. In addition to helping on the family farm, poorer women had to perform many menial tasks, such as cooking, cleaning, spinning, and weaving. If a woman did not marry she remained under the control of her father or brothers.

ALEXANDER THE GREAT (356-323 BCE)

Alexander became king of Macedon at the age of 20. He went on to become one of the world's greatest leaders. He achieved what no other Greek leader had accomplished, in uniting all the individual city-states into one nation. He built an empire that stretched from Italy in the west, Kashmir in the east and Egypt in the south. He died in Babylon aged just 32. Without his firm leadership, the alliances that he forged between the various city-states weakened and in a short while Alexander's empire collapsed.

STRONGHOLDS

At the center, and usually the highest point of every Greek town was a fortified citadel known as an acropolis. Strong walls and gat protected the main temples and other important buildings from attack in the event of an invasion.

NAVAL POWER

The Greeks relied heavily on the strength of their fleet in retaining mastery of the Aegean Sea, particularly important as many Greek colonies were situated on islands. The fastest and most powerful Greek ship was the *trireme*, which was powered by three tiers of oarsmen, one above the other, on either side. A metal-pointed battering ram was attached to the bows to ram and sink enemy ships.

CHARIOTS

Chariots first appeared in Sumeria and Egypt around 3000 BCE. They were small two-wheeled carts pulled by horses and carried two men, a driver and an armed soldier. The Greek army made great use of them, charging the enemy lines and throwing them into disarray.

THE TROJAN WAR

Sieges could last many years, as in the case of Troy (*c.* 1184 BCE) which lasted 10 years. The usual practice was to burn the crops surrounding a city and cut off all other supply routes to deny food to the defenders. The combined Greek army eventually won by trickery. Soldiers concealed inside a huge wooden horse, supposedly left behind as a gift to the Trojans, opened the city gates at night letting in the Greek army.

War & Weaponry

Unlike other great civilizations, ancient Greece was never a unified country. For complex reasons of geography and culture, the region developed as a series of independent city-states. Although each of these mini-states was influenced by the others, they were often fiercely independent. Quarrels and wars between the individual states were commonplace and each seems to have taken it in turn to become the most dominant and powerful state. When a war was waged, every male citizen had a duty to help fight, as there were no permanent armies, except in Sparta. After the crisis, they returned to their usual work.

On only three occasions did the various Greek states unite to act together: notably, the Trojan wars of the late 12th century BCE; the Persian wars of the 6th and 5th centuries BCE; and lastly by Alexander the Great, in the 4th century BCE. On the first two occasions they did so out of fear of being conquered. On the last occasion, Alexander united the states by force in order to fulfil his plans of building a Greek empire.

GREEK FIRE

This vase decoration shows Odysseus, a legendary Greek hero, returning from war. Greek ships (called galleys) were quite large and often carried siege engines, such as catapults and ballistas, which could throw projectiles weighing up to 55 pounds. Sometimes, burning missiles made from naphtha, sulfur and saltpeter (known as "Greek Fire") were hurled amongst enemy ships.

MILITARY SERVICE

There was no standing army in Greece (except in Sparta), but men were trained from age 20 and could be drafted in to do military service at any time. Foot soldiers, known as Hoplites, paid for their own equipment which usually consisted of a short sword and spear, with a bronze shield, breastplate and helmet for protection.

Crime & Punishment

Because ancient Greece was not a unified country with one central system of government, it is difficult for us today to understand the complex systems of government and law that operated within the various city-states. Some states, like Lesbos, adopted a much more liberal attitude than more military states, such as Sparta, and this was reflected in their laws. In Athens the ruling classes were driven out and replaced with a democratic system of government and law making. Although only certain classes of citizens had the right to vote, ordinary people were able to make decisions about government for themselves at meetings called "assemblies." Not all Greek states adopted the democratic system, however, and many people stood out against it, including the philosopher, Plato. Greece eventually reverted to a monarchical system of government. In the 6th century BCE, Solon, a member of the Athens Council, introduced a law giving ordinary citizens the right of appeal against judiciary decisions. By all accounts though, the crime rate generally in Greece was low.

BANKRUPTCY

If a farmer fell upon hard times and got into debt (which happened frequently in ancient Greece when crops often failed in the poor soils) his possessions could be seized and he could be sold into slavery as a bankrupt.

The Athenian politician Solon (c.640-558 BCE) shown above, introduced new laws abolishing this practice.

SACRED TEMPLES

To most Greeks, religion was intrinsically entwined with everyday life. The defiling of temples such as this magnificent temple of Apollo in Delphi would have been considered a crime against the entire community. The ultimate fulfilment in life was to serve one's own community and so the ultimate deterrent and punishment for many crimes was banishment, to deny the criminal all the benefits of the Greek way of life. Some crimes, however, such as murder and corruption, were punishable by execution.

DEATH BY POISONING

The teachings of the philosopher Socrates (470-399 BCE) were considered so outrageous, even for liberal-minded Greeks, that both government and temple officials considered him a corrupting influence on the young. One principle advanced by him, and copied by Nazi Germany in this century, was selective breeding to produce a super race. He was eventually arrested for his controversial views and was sentenced to death by drinking hemlock.

OSTRACISM

Citizens in the city-state of Athens reserved the right to punish any politician who they thought had behaved badly by banishing them for 10 years. Citizens would cast a vote of no-confidence by writing the person's name on a piece of pottery (as shown here) called an *ostrakon*. The pieces were then counted and if they numbered more than 6,000 the named person was banished. This process was called "ostracising" and is a term still used today.

PERIKLES

Although Athens adopted the democratic system of government, it did not meet with universal approval. The system was still dominated by powerful statesmen, who could force through laws of their own choosing. The illustration shows Perikles, who was elected "strategos" (leader of the military) for 14 years in succession, between 443-429 BCE.

Transport & Science

The Greeks were greatly influenced by the Egyptians, particularly in scientific studies. The sciences then embraced such subjects as religion, the arts philosophy, math, astronomy and astrology, and it is in these areas that the Greeks still affect modern thought today. Perhaps the strongest area of influence, after the arts, has been in philosophical debate. The Greek philosophers were visionary, as were the mathematicians who developed theories concerning atomic principles, before they knew that atoms actually existed. Astronomers also introduced revolutionary theories. As long ago as the 6th century BCE, Anaxagoras discovered that the moon did not emanate light, but merely reflected that of the sun. Whilst 300 years later Aristarchus recognized that the Sun, not the Earth, was the center of our solar system.

ROAD TO NOWHERE

Most Greek towns were well serviced with paved roads. These were built with drainage channels and pavements for pedestrians. Some of the earliest examples of roads are to be found in Crete. The example shown here is the Lechaian Road in Corinth. On mainland Greece there were a few long-distance roads, but hardly any linking up the various towns. The mountains made such an enterprise very difficult. For long journeys most Greeks used boats to move around the coast and avoid the hazards of mountain tracks.

MARITIME POWER

Because of its lack of natural resources, Greece relied heavily on trade. Most of the major cities were located on islands scattered across the Aegean and control of the trade routes by sea was essential to maintain the empire.

PLATO

One of the foremost Greek philosophers was Plato (*c.*427-347 BCE), who wrote several books discussing the origins of the universe and the relationship between man and the natural world. He lived in Athens and set up a school for philosophers. In addition to teaching (much of which was done by open discussion rather than by lecturing) he also wrote down many of the teachings of Socrates, a fellow philosopher who never actually committed his ideas to paper, preferring the medium of debate.

SEAWORTHY

Sometime around 1600 BCE the Minoan civilization, centered on the island of Crete, dramatically improved ship design, making long sea voyages possible. The ships were propelled by the combined use of oars and sails, the manpower usually provided by slaves. Higher prows enabled the ships to cut through the water more easily and a large oar was placed at the stern to act as a rudder.

PYTHAGORAS

To the ancient Greeks, science and religion were inextricably linked, so too were an understanding of art and philosophy. Pythagoras (*c.*580-500 BCE) was born on the island of Samos and devoted his life to the study of mathematics. Amongst his theories was the idea that all things in the cosmos were determined by numbers and mathematical relationships. He developed many mathematical principles, especially in geometry, which are still in use today.

TIME-HONORED TRADITION

This modern photograph shows a peasant woman on the island of Crete leading a donkey along a pack trail. Scenes such as this have hardly changed for centuries. Beasts of burden, such as the donkey, were essential for transport in ancient Greece, where mountain communities were cut off from one another and only accessible along narrow tracks.

PAN

Pan was one of the minor gods. The son of Hermes, he was half-man, half-goat, and the god of shepherds and flocks. He invented the pan-pipes and loved to spend time in the forest, hunting and dancing. A mischievous god, he apparently liked to startle unwary travelers and "panic" them.

KING OF THE GODS

Cronos, youngest son of Uranos (Heaven), is said to have revolted against his father and married his sister, Rhea. To prevent his own sons deposing him he ate each of his children at birth. When Zeus was born, Rhea wanted to save her son and gave Cronos a stone to swallow instead. When he came of age Zeus moved to Mount Olympus, near Macedonia. The twelve main Greek gods all resided on Olympia. Zeus became the king of the gods, and his symbol was thunder.

GODDESS ATHENA

Athena was the daughter of Zeus and Metis. She was the goddess of wisdom and warfare. She was often accompanied by an owl and presided over the arts, literature, learning, and philosophy. She became the patron goddess of Athens, the most powerful Greek city-state (which was so named in honor of her). The temple of the Parthenon in Athens is dedicated to her.

TEMPLES OF THE GODS

Each of the various Greek gods had their own special attributes and were worshipped in their own temple. By appeasing the gods, making offerings or animal sacrifices, believers hoped to win their favor. Greek towns had many fine temples, each one splendidly decorated. Worshippers usually made individual offerings rather than attend organized services.

Religion

Greek religion was polytheistic, that is they believed in many gods, not just one. The Greeks invented a very complex mythology to explain both the creation of the universe and the origins of the various gods. They saw the world before creation as Chaos, from which sprang the Earth (Ge, or Gaia), who gave birth to the Heavens (Uranos) and the sea (Pontus). The gods were human-like beings who resided on Mount Olympus, and frequently intervened in the affairs of man. Greek religion did not have a moral code. People simply had to appease the gods to get what they wanted from life. If offended, the gods might punish people, but it was not necessary to live a "good" life in order to be a believer or to receive favor from the gods.

THE FALL OF ICARUS

Daedalus was a mythical craftsman, responsible for many advances in architecture and sculpture. After he killed his nephew, Talos, in a jealous rage, he fled Athens for Crete with his son Icarus. They were later imprisoned by King Minos. They escaped using wings, fastened to their shoulders with wax, but Icarus flew too close to the sun, melting the wax, and he fell into the sea and drowned.

SON OF ZEUS

Heracles, perhaps the greatest of all heroes, was the son of Zeus by a mortal woman, Alcmene. Although Heracles never became a god himself, he frequently called upon them for their help. He is most famous for his Twelve Labors. When he died he was carried by a cloud to Olympus, where he became immortal and lived with the gods.

GODDESS OF LOVE

The relief above shows Aphrodite the goddess of love, desire, and fertility. According to legend she was born out of the sea, either from drops of Uranos's blood, falling from the heavens, or from the union of Zeus and Diane. She possessed a magic girdle, which if given to a mortal made the wearer irresistibly beautiful and desirable.

Legacy of the Past

The civilization that was ancient Greece was by no means the first great civilization; Sumeria, India and Egypt had already flourished and gone into decline long before the founding of the first Greek city-state. However, the founding of Minoan Crete was the first early civilization in Europe. Greek culture flourished around the Aegean Sea, on mainland Greece and eastern Turkey, and on the many islands of the eastern Mediterranean. However, because their civilization was made up of individual city-states, it meant they were often fiercely independent. Had the Greeks ever formed a unified empire they may well have established an even greater civilization. It reached its zenith in the 5th century BCE, leaving behind a magnificent legacy of art and architecture, scientific and scholarly research, sports, medicine, philosophy, and a system of government, all of which still form the basis of life today.

THE RENAISSANCE

In 17th-century Europe many architects rejected medieval ideals in building design and looked to the grandeur and elegance of classical Greece as their source of inspiration. The period came to be known as the Renaissance, or "re-birth."

THE OLYMPIC GAMES

The sporting ideals created by the Greeks at their great games (particularly the Olympics) live on today. They first developed the idea that it is more important to compete and gain honor for one's community than it is to win.

DEMOCRACY

The governments of the Western world today are founded on the basic principles of democracy, from the Greek words "demos," meaning people, and "krakos," meaning power. Democracy was first developed in Athens in the 5th century BCE, when a monarchical system of government was replaced by one with elected representatives. The system was not universally supported, however, and not everyone was represented; women, for example, were excluded from voting.

THE ROMAN EMPIRE

The Romans greatly respected the Greeks, modeling their own civilization upon theirs. They especially admired the magnificent yet simple elegance of Greek architecture and used it as the basis for their own style, as can be seen from the Colosseum in Rome.

THE ELGIN MARBLES

For centuries the magnificent remains of classical Greece lay unprotected and uncared for and locals used the buildings as convenient stone quarries. During the 18th and, more particularly, the 19th centuries interest in the ancient world was revived and many sites were excavated. A great many statues and artefacts were rescued and placed in museums around the world. Lord Elgin, a British ambassador, brought back several large sculptures from the Parthenon, in Athens. They can still be seen in the British Museum today.

THEATER-GOING

Theater-going was probably started by the ancient Greeks and has remained a popular form of entertainment since those times. Modern theater design is still based on Greek models with a curved auditorium and seats rising in tiers from front to back.

HERITAGE

Perhaps the ancient Greek's finest legacy is the wealth of art and architectural remains which are a source of inspiration to us today. Sadly, many of these remains have been lost, buried beneath modern towns or deliberately destroyed for the sake of their materials, but enough survives for us to form a picture of the earliest (and some would say greatest) civilization in Europe.

Who were the Ancient Romans?

The emergence of ancient Rome as a power in the Mediterranean was a long, slow process and owed much to the Greek civilization that preceded it. The lands around the Mediterranean were not unified under a central political system, but consisted of a number of independent city-states; self-governing regions comprising a large town, several villages and the lands between. By tradition, the small city-state of Rome was said to be created in 753 BCE. Its inhabitants were a mixture of Etruscans (who ruled over much of Italy) and Latins (from southern Italy). They collectively became known as Romans. From about 550 BCE Rome was ruled by Etruscan kings, but in 509 BCE the Romans drove the king out and Rome became a tiny, independent republic.

HIGH STANDARD OF LIVING

With the expansion of the Roman Empire came great wealth. Riches were brought from abroad, along with slaves to do the menial tasks. This meant that the average Roman lived comfortably, with a minority living extremely well.

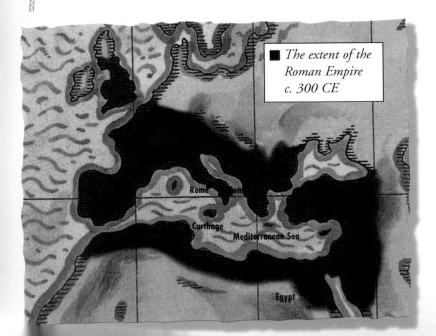

The extent of the Roman Empire c. 300 CE

Rome

Carthage

Mediterranean Sea

Egypt

A NIGHT ON THE TOWN

The Romans learnt much from Greek architecture but went on to develop their own style. They perfected the semi-circular arch which allowed them to build higher, more magnificent structures, many of which are still standing today. Most Roman towns had huge amphitheaters for the entertainment of the masses, where they staged plays, sporting events and even blood sports.

THE MIGHT OF ROME

The strength and growth
of the Roman Empire lay
with its military efficiency.
The Romans were able
to organize a centrally
controlled army, something
no other civilization had
managed. Divided into
legions of about 5,000
men, the army was
well equipped and very
disciplined compared with
its adversaries who still
fought in small, disorganized
bands. Few armies could
resist the might of the
Roman legions.

ROMULUS & REMUS

According to legend, the state of Rome was founded by the
twin brothers Romulus and Remus. They were said to be
descendants of the Roman god Mars and Rhea Silvia,
daughter of Numitor, king of Alba Lenga. The twins were
thrown into the River Tiber by a wicked great uncle, hoping they
would drown. Fortunately they were washed ashore and were saved by a she-wolf
(as depicted here). A shepherd raised them and later they were reunited with their
grandfather, King Numitor. As adults, they quarreled over who should rule Rome, the
city they had both founded. Romulus killed Remus in 753 BCE to become king. The clan
of Romulus were Latins, from Latium, a district
south and west of the River Tiber and its valley.

STRUCTURED SOCIETY

Roman society was very structured. Young men were encouraged
to learn a trade or join the army; women to create a stable family
background. Although people were mostly illiterate, writing was
encouraged in wealthy and political circles to record the greatness of
the empire. Latin, the basis for many modern languages, became the
language of the Romans as the Etruscan language died out.

HEARTH & HOME

The typical house of a wealthy Roman contained an impressive entrance vestibule, called an atrium, which was often open to the sky and may have had a fountain or pool as a central feature. It would also include a *lararium*, as shown here, which was a household shrine to worship domestic gods and godesses, such as the goddess of the hearth, Vesta.

LITERACY

Many nobles could read and write having been educated by private tutors as children. The girl shown above is using a stylus to inscribe a wax tablet. Romans also wrote with metal nibbed or hollow reed pens on papyrus paper or vellum (stretched animal skin).

HOME COMFORTS

Many of the richest Roman citizens had two houses, a town house and a country villa. Furnishings were kept simple and decoration was plain, yet elegant. Larger Roman houses had few windows, to keep out the heat of the sun, and usually had at least one open courtyard, complete with fountain. Floors and walls were kept cool with the prodigious use of marble or stone tiles, often inlaid with elaborate mosaics, as shown here.

TAKING IT EASY

This elegant couch was used to recline on for an afternoon nap. It would also have been used at mealtimes to seat two or three guests. Food would have been placed on low tables with several such seats arranged around them.

Life for the Rich

A great many of the things we usually associate with the Romans, such as their luxurious lifestyle, are better associated with the rich than with Romans in general. As in most societies of the past, the artefacts which have survived the passage of time are not necessarily those which best represent that society. The items shown on these pages would have been known to a comparative few: the rich and elite of society. The high standard and sheer quality are a testament to the heights of sophistication reached by Roman civilization. In many cases such standards of living were not achieved again until the late 19th century.

The larger houses had their own plumbed water supply and many were also furnished with a hypocaust—underfloor central heating.

A STABLE SOCIETY

The Roman Empire, for a time at least, brought peace and stability to central and southern Europe (a period known as the Roman Peace), and with it came prosperity, certainly for the ruling classes. Roman coinage was distributed throughout the empire to provide a common monetary unit and make trade between the member nations easier.

SOCIAL STANDING

Roman society made great use of slavery. Unfortunate prisoners captured from conquered lands were put to work as menial laborers or were employed as servants in wealthy households. Society was divided into tiers, comprising citizens; non-citizens (or provincials), who had fewer rights; and slaves, who had no rights at all.

THE FORUM

The central meeting place in a typical Roman town was called the forum, from the Latin word *foris*, which means "outside." It began as a simple open space where weekly markets were held. Forums evolved into important centers of commerce, where the wealthy conducted their business.

Life for the Poor

The Roman world was full of contradictions and paradoxes. Its culture was one of the most sophisticated; its society one of the richest ever known, providing untold wealth and splendor for some. However, for most people life was oppressive. The increasing cost of maintaining the empire placed an excessive tax demand on all classes. The poor strongly resented the leisurely and flamboyant lifestyles of the rich. There was no infrastructure of social care in Roman society; the poor were largely left to fend for themselves as best they could. There were few means of escape from poverty. Young men might have considered a career in either the priesthood or the army, both of which provided regular work and money. For girls, usually the only salvation was to attract a rich husband.

CREATURE COMFORTS

The poor had few comforts or luxuries. Housing conditions were usually squalid, with no sanitation. There were public baths, but they were not free and rarely could the very poor afford them. Town dwellers often had to use public toilet facilities. Water was at least clean and free, collected from public fountains. Lighting was normally by oil lamps (shown above) burning olive oil.

LIFE IN THE TOWNS

In the towns most poor people lived in cramped, low-quality tenement housing. Several stories of apartments were built over open-fronted shops or workshops. Few people in towns provided their own food, they bought their supplies from country people who took any excess they had to market. Townspeople usually earned their living providing a service or trade, working in shops, or as clerks for the Roman civil service. The picture shows the remains of a typical town street in Pompeii, in south-west Italy.

LIFE IN THE COUNTRY

Most country dwellers were poor, eking out a subsistence living on small family farms. Cows were kept for their milk (to drink and to make into cheese). Poultry was kept for eggs. Meat was only occasionally served at table. All members of the family were expected to work, including the children. The men looked after the livestock and carried out heavy tasks, such as plowing. Women tended the crops, looked after the house and family, and made clothes. The children would help with domestic chores and wherever they could around the farm.

SUBSISTENCE FARMING

By today's standards, Roman farming methods were quite primitive and inefficient, though by the standards of their day Roman agriculture was superior to most other Mediterranean countries. The Romans invented a new form of plow, using a strong metal blade to replace its wood or bone predecessor. It was able

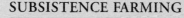

to cut a deeper furrow, very important when farming in the poor infertile soils of hot countries. Sugar was unknown in the Roman world so bees were kept to manufacture honey as a sweetener.

FAMILY LIFE

Family life was very important to the Romans, whether rich or poor. There were no pensions so the responsibility for looking after elderly relatives fell on the entire family. Most people continued working until they were either too frail, or died.

Food & Drink

By all accounts Romans from all classes ate and drank comparatively well. Their diet was probably very similar to that still enjoyed in many parts of the Mediterranean today, consisting of plenty of fresh fruit and vegetables, supplemented by fish and poultry. Red meat was seldom eaten in Roman society. Salads were common at mealtimes and were often used as a garnish, since the look of a dish was just as important to Romans as its taste. Even the poor were better nourished than their contemporaries in other regions of the known world. Their staple diet was bread and vegetables and their main meal would have taken place after the day's work. For the rich, mealtimes were an excuse for social gatherings, starting in the middle of the afternoon and continuing over several hours. Cooking utensils and pots were usually made of bronze for the wealthy, or earthenware for the poor. They ate with knives only, so finger bowls were provided to keep hands clean.

THE SPICE OF LIFE

Roman housewives would be familiar with many of the herbs used by modern cooks to add flavor and interest to their meals, such as parsley, thyme, fennel, fenugreek, angelica, and mint. Spices, imported from the East, were used to disguise the often rancid taste of food, particularly meat, that might not keep well in the Mediterranean heat.

SERVING VESSELS

Romans used a variety of vessels both to serve and drink wine. Jugs and wine cups were made out of pottery, bronze or glass (as shown here), or even finely engraved silver.

EVERYDAY DRINKS

The usual drink for Romans of all classes was wine; the wealthy simply drank better quality wine. Despite their care in providing fresh water supplies, water-borne diseases such as cholera could still cause epidemics, so it was safer to drink alcohol. There is no evidence that Romans drank hot drinks, other than mulled wine. To reduce the effects of drunkenness, wine was always mixed with water. It was considered improper to drink wine neat.

OLIVES

One of the principal crops grown in the Roman world was olives, as it still is in many Mediterranean regions today. Olives had many uses. They were eaten whole, as appetizers, or crushed for their oil. The oil was extracted by pressing the fruits, in much the same way as grapes for wine-making. The oil was as versatile as it was valuable. It was used for cooking and salad dressings; for burning in lamps; for massaging into the skin as a beauty aid, and for anointing the dead.

HOME COOKING

At Pompeii, much of the ordinary domestic architecture of the Romans remains preserved beneath the ashes. This impressive stone oven is just such an example and shows how most Roman women probably cooked their meals. The central hearth was fueled by wood or charcoal. The individual round openings on the top were probably covered by grills to allow several pans to be used at once.

GOD OF WINE

Bacchus was the Roman god of wine. Vineyards existed outside most towns, and wealthy citizens frequently had their own private vineyards. Roman wine came in four main varieties: black, red, yellow and white, both dry and sweet. They frequently mixed it with other ingredients such as herbs or honey, particularly older wines to make them more palatable. The sour grapes were often used to make verjuice, a mild vinegar used for salad dressings, sauces and marinades.

THEATRICS

Romans were great theatergoers. Most towns had an amphitheater, usually open to the sky, so most performances took place during the day. Only men could become actors (women's roles were played by boys) and each character wore a mask to represent their character.

BLOOD SPORTS

Romans loved to watch blood sports. The entertainment at arenas was usually organized by the emperor or other dignitaries to win popularity. They usually went on all day. First, wild animals such as lions and tigers were brought in to kill one another (at the inauguration of the Colosseum, 5,000 wild animals were slaughtered in a single day). This progressed to pitting defenseless slaves or religious martyrs against the animals. Condemned criminals had to fight one another and contests usually went on to the death.

CHARIOT RACING

Most of the larger Roman towns had a stadium, (an elongated arena) where chariot races were staged. Small, two-wheeled carts were pulled by two to four horses at great speed around a track. The excitement was intense as the public bet on the outcome. Accidents were common, frequently resulting in death.

THE COLOSSEUM

The Colosseum in Rome was the greatest amphitheater ever built. Unlike other theaters it seems not to have been designed for the performances of plays, but for spectator sports to amuse the crowds. It was built to a brilliant design and was free standing (most amphitheaters were built into natural depressions in hillsides), and it could seat 50,000 people. Its specially constructed floor could be filled with water to allow the enactment of sea battles.

Pastimes

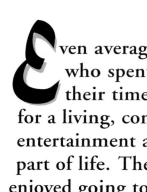

Even average Romans, who spent most of their time working for a living, considered entertainment an essential part of life. They regularly enjoyed going to the theater, or to the arena to watch sporting events. The Romans had many gods to worship so there was almost always a feast day to celebrate, many of which became a good excuse for a festival of music and dance. Rich nobles preferred to hire musicians to play at their private banquets rather than join in large public displays. The wealthy also spent a great deal of time going to the baths, where they met friends, exchanged gossip, and enjoyed the waters.

AN EAR FOR MUSIC

Music accompanied most religious ceremonies or events at the arena, though dancing was usually reserved for the poorer classes. Instruments were quite simple, such as flutes, pan pipes, and lyres (shown here being played by Apollo, the Roman god of light, poetry, and music).

GLADIATORS

The most spectacular event at the Colosseum was watching the gladiators fight to the death. Gladiators were usually criminals or slaves and were trained to fight in special schools. Occasionally, women were trained to become gladiators.

Fashion

The Roman Empire spanned nearly 700 years (though there were periods of ascendancy and decline) which meant that fashions changed quite considerably, though the change was probably gradual from generation to generation. Children did not have their own fashions, as now, but wore clothes that were miniature copies of adult clothes. Because of the hot climate, the emphasis was on keeping cool. Generally, light materials were used, which might have included silks from China or cotton from India, for those who could afford these expensive imports. Both men and women were quite fastidious about their appearance. In general, light colors (often white) were preferred. The color purple, still associated with royalty, was first adopted by the Romans as a symbol of power. It was the most expensive clothes dye to produce. Officials wore togas with a purple stripe, but only the emperor could wear a totally purple toga.

FOOT LOOSE

Both men and women favored open sandals, for ventilation in the hot sun. They came in various styles, but were usually flat, or with very low heels. The thongs and straps were made of leather. The soles were usually made of shaped wood (or heavy hide), sometimes with studs for longer wear.

MIRROR, MIRROR

Because the technique of manufacturing mirror glass had not yet been perfected, the Romans made mirrors by highly polishing pieces of metal, usually silver or bronze. This beautiful example was finely engraved on the reverse side.

CHANGING FACE OF FASHION

Roman women favored coiffured hairstyles, pinned back and held in place with a comb. It was fashionable for women to keep a pale complexion, difficult in the Mediterranean sun. Many women covered their faces as much as possible, while others applied chalk dust as a face powder.

LOOKING GOOD

Women of all classes wore jewelry. Those who could afford it wore gold and silver necklaces, bracelets and earrings, decorated with jewels or rare stones. Bronze was used as a cheaper substitute, embellished with colored glass beads to resemble jewels, rather in the manner of costume jewelry today. Both men and women wore rings. Perfumes were widely available, mostly made from plant extracts.

THE TOGA

The toga was the national dress of Rome and it was the right of all free-born citizens to wear it. But contrary to popular belief, the toga was normally worn only on special or formal occasions, and then usually only by the rich. It was heavy and cumbersome. For normal everyday wear tunics were worn by men and women. Trousers or leggings were considered unmanly and uncivilized. Poorer classes wore similar fashions, but made from inferior materials.

FOLLOWERS OF FASHION

Early in the period, men sported long hair and curly beards, in the Greek fashion, but by the end of the Roman era a clean-shaven, cropped look was fashionable. Although individual fashion styles changed considerably during the course of the Roman era, the basic design of clothes remained unchanged. Both men and women wore loose-fitting garments rather than being tailored to fit. Underwear was worn, but again, this was loose-fitting. Tunics were usually cut from one large piece of material, fastened at the shoulder by a brooch (as shown here) or a decorative pin.

WALL PAINTINGS

Most Roman buildings, especially the villas of the wealthy and the interiors of temples, were decorated with fine wall murals, usually depicting scenes from mythology or the exploits of the gods. They were usually painted directly onto the plaster so few have survived, but those that have display a vivid realism.

Art & Architecture

The Romans copied, or adapted, many Greek architectural styles, adding their own embellishments and improving the designs. They made greater use of arches than the Greeks, developing the semi-circular arch. Although massively constructed, such techniques allowed the Romans to build higher and on a grander scale than had previously been possible. By adding a volcanic material called *pozzolana* (and other minerals) to their cement they also created an incredibly strong form of concrete, stronger even than the materials it bonded together. This enabled masons to build strong walls at a much quicker rate than before, comprising an outer and inner wall of dressed stones with rubble in-fill.

The Romans built on a monumental scale and decorated the interiors of their buildings with polished marble, fine mosaics, and paintings.

HEIGHTS OF PERFECTION

The Romans achieved greater heights for their buildings by erecting walls with several tiers of arches (see picture of the aqueduct on page 79). They also developed the semi-circular arch and invented the dome, enabling them to roof buildings in stone.

MOSAICS

Many Roman buildings were decorated with mosaics on the floor or walls. Mosaics are pictures made by carefully laying small, brightly painted and enameled squared stones into wet plaster to form a picture or decorative design. They were also extremely hard-wearing and many have survived. Skilled mosaic layers called on wealthy villa owners with pattern books from which they chose a design.

FORTIFICATIONS

The Romans built massive fortifications to protect their empire, either in the form of strong city walls or forts to protect their legions. In Britain, to defend their northernmost outpost from attacks by the Scots, the Emperor Hadrian built a huge defensive wall right across the country from east to west. It was 75 miles (120 km) long, 15 feet (4.6 meters) high, and 10 feet (3 meters) thick. Much of it still survives today.

TOOLS OF THE TRADE

These tools were used by a Roman stonemason and are similar to those still in use today. On the left is a bronze square for measuring 45° and 90° angles. The dividers (right) were used to transfer measurements from scaled building plans directly onto stone. They were especially used to create intricate carvings.

EPHESUS

The Roman remains at Ephesus in western Turkey are amongst the finest to be seen anywhere. Although the Romans admired the elegant lines of Greek architecture, as their empire expanded and they took over Greek territories, they often replaced Greek buildings with their own, as at Ephesus. Many of the civic buildings survive at Ephesus, including the library of Celsius, shown here.

Health & Medicine

ROMAN BATHS

Water supplies in the Roman world were very sophisticated and were not improved upon in Europe until the 19th century. Most towns had public water fountains, bath houses and toilets. Romans also recognized the health benefits of hot and cold plunge baths to purge and revitalize the system. These shown here are at Bath, in England.

Although the Romans understood the importance of personal hygiene, clean water, and drainage systems to prevent disease, their knowledge of medicine was still somewhat primitive. They were a superstitious people who largely believed that diseases were a curse, given by the gods who had been in some way offended. Because of this, many people sought cures by supernatural means, by visiting healing shrines or by carrying lucky talismans to ward off evil spirits. Most physicians were Greek and they relied heavily upon herbal remedies, which were quite effective for most everyday ailments. There were no cures for more serious complaints. Surgery was basic and crudely executed, without any form of anesthetic. Many operations were amputations or for wounds sustained in battle. Most legions had their own doctors who traveled with them to tend to the wounded, many of whom died even after treatment from secondary infections or gangrene.

HEALING HANDS

This detail from a wall mural shows Aeneas, a legendary war hero, having an arrow-head removed from his leg by a surgeon. Antiseptic ointments, made from herbs such as thyme, were applied in the form of a poultice. Even so, it was common for wounds to become infected or turn gangrenous, resulting in amputation, or even death, from quite minor injuries.

THE APPLIANCE OF SCIENCE

This collection of surgical instruments was in use throughout the Roman period and is not too dissimilar to those still used up until the 19th century. It includes knives and scalpels for making incisions, hooks to manipulate blood vessels and organs during an operation and spatulas for mixing and applying ointments or for internal examinations. Human anatomy was little understood and many patients died from shock or trauma on the operating table.

FRESH WATER

Romans developed a way to bring in fresh water supplies across deep valleys, as shown by this impressive aqueduct at Nimes, in France. Water was carried in a covered channel built into the top tier.

PERSONAL HYGIENE

This fragment of a hair comb is made of ivory and is inscribed with a relief depicting a religious ceremony. It probably belonged to a rich person, but even the poor were fastidious about their personal hygiene and used combs made of wood or bone to remove head lice.

NATURE'S CURE-ALL

The use of garlic for medicinal purposes had been widespread probably since ancient Egyptian times. It was also claimed to have the power to remove evil spirits so, to the Romans, it was doubly effective. They used it as a purgative to cleanse the system, and crushed it was an antiseptic ointment for wounds and the treatment of leprosy. Soldiers were given a daily dose to improve their general well-being.

CLEAN WATER SUPPLIES

The Romans developed a sophisticated system of water supply. Clean water was collected in huge reservoirs in the countryside, and piped into smaller feeder tanks in the towns. They also recognized the importance of keeping drinking water well away from drainage systems to prevent disease.

GOD OF FERTILITY

Bacchus, the Roman god of wine, was also the god of fertility (after the Greek Dionysus). He is often associated with merry-making and wedding feasts. Festivities would often degenerate into rowdiness and unrestrained merry-making, as shown in this sarcophagus frieze.

CUPID'S ARROW

Cupid (known to the Greeks as Eros) was the son of Venus. He was the winged god of love who carried a magical bow and arrow. If Cupid fired an arrow into the hearts of a man and a woman they were said to fall hopelessly in love with one another.

THE WEDDING CEREMONY

This figurine shows the goddess Vesta giving her blessing to a wedding ceremony. As goddess of the hearth, it was customary to make offerings to Vesta (and other gods) to ensure a happy family life after marriage. Sometimes this might take the form of an animal sacrifice.

Often the wedding ceremony took place at the home of the bride's parents.

THE GODDESS OF LOVE

The Greek goddess of love and beauty was Aphrodite, whom the Romans renamed Venus. She is nearly always shown naked, or semi-clothed, and depicte as a beautiful young woman In Roman mythology, Venu was the divine ancestor of Julius Caesar's family, which caused many to resent them because of their supposed familiarity with the gods. It was considered good luck to bless her altar on th wedding day because she wa also the goddess of fertility. She possessed a magic girdle which reputedly made the wearer irresistibly attractive.

GIRL POWER

This detail from a frieze at Pompeii, in the "Villa of Mysteries," shows a young woman's initiation into religious mysteries. Unlike men who became priests and were allowed to marry, women who entered the priesthood were expected to remain virgins and unmarried.

Love & Marriage

Many of today's marriage ceremonies and rituals are derived from the Romans. A wedding ring, for example, (usually plain to symbolize virtue) was placed on the third finger of the left hand because a nerve was thought to run from there directly to the heart. The bride wore a white toga with a colored veil, and a feast was held at the house of the bride's father where a wedding cake was served to the guests. Marriages were usually arranged between both sets of parents and girls could be married as young as thirteen; boys were usually a little older. The girl's parents were normally expected to give a dowry of money and goods to the groom's family. Most women were considered to be the property of their husbands and regained their property only on his death. Understandably most chose not to remarry.

DUTIFUL WIVES

Women were expected to be dutiful wives and mothers. The more wealthy were allowed greater freedom, but most were expected to obey their husbands. Disobedience would normally be punished. This wall painting from the 1st century CE shows the everyday appearance of a wealthy married couple.

DEVOTED COUPLE

The Greek colony of Etruria in northern Italy was instrumental in the founding of Rome and greatly influenced Roman civilization. This magnificent Etruscan sarcophagus dating back to the 6th century BCE comes from the tomb of a devoted husband and wife who share the same grave.

Women & Children

MIDWIFERY

One of the few occupations nearing a profession that was open to women was midwifery. Giving birth was dangerous and many babies and mothers died. The Romans are thought to have first performed a Caesarean section operation when Julius Caesar was born by this method. His name is thought to have come from the Latin word *caesus*, meaning "cut."

As in most other civilizations of the past, life for Roman women was hard. Women experienced a great deal of prejudice and were usually regarded as second-class citizens in Roman society. Wealth determined the amount of freedom and independence a woman might enjoy. Most were expected to keep house for the family, work in the fields and tend to such mundane jobs as spinning and weaving. Only wealthy children were educated, usually by private tutors or, more rarely, by attending school. Girls were usually only educated to a very basic standard and were then expected to learn domestic duties. Only boys were educated beyond that and groomed for a profession. Poor women were usually confined to working in the fields or becoming servants. Those slightly more well-off might secure a job in a shop, or become hairdressers. The lucky few might become a priestess (such as tending the shrine of the Vestal Virgins) but openings were few, and only for the rich.

WORKING ON THE LAND

The majority of country dwellers eked out a subsistence standard of living off the land. The Romans developed more efficient methods of agriculture but life was still hard, each family tending its own animals and crops. Most of the menial jobs were performed by women and children. These included sowing seeds, tending the crops, feeding the poultry, collecting the eggs, milking the cows, and making cheese.

PLAYTHINGS

Children played with a variety of toys, some of which were quite sophisticated. These pieces are from a game similar to dominoes. Boys might have played with lead soldiers and marbles, while girls had rag dolls.

THE VESTAL VIRGINS

Only rich women could become priestesses and then only for certain gods and goddesses. The cult of Vesta was particularly associated with women. Granted the gift of perpetual virginity, her shrine and holy flame in Rome was attended by a select group of priestesses known as the Vestal Virgins.

JUNO

The patron goddess of women was Juno, one of Jupiter's consorts (the other was Minerva). She is normally shown seated, as in this fine terracotta statue, usually accompanied by a peacock, her symbol. She is a very maternal figure, the protectress of women, especially during childbirth. Originally, she was the goddess of the moon, the queen of heaven.

SONG & DANCE

Isis was an Egyptian god adopted by the Romans, and is particularly associated with women and children and the cycle of life. This relief, probably from a child's sarcophagus, was found south of Rome and shows women and children dancing as part of a religious ritual to Isis.

CHILDHOOD

This child wears a *bulla* (lucky charm) around his neck, which would have been given to him at a naming ceremony conducted a few days after his birth. The inscription below includes a dedication to the spirits of the dead, which indicates that this a relief from the child's tomb. Child mortality was high with only half expected to reach age 20.

War & Weaponry

From the 8th century BCE until about 509 BCE, Rome was ruled by her Etruscan neighbors in the north. When Rome became a republic in that year, the Romans removed the Etruscan king, Tarquin the Proud, from office and ruled themselves. Rome's power gradually grew to take control of much of Italy. Around 260 BCE, Rome clashed with Carthage, a north-African state, so beginning a century of bitter wars. When Rome emerged victorious in 146 BCE it had acquired its first overseas dominions. In order to gain victory, Rome had to organize a highly disciplined army, which then went on to conquer neighboring lands. By 50 CE most of the Mediterranean basin had fallen to the might of the Roman legions.

AUGUSTUS
63 BCE-14 CE

Caesar's adopted son Octavian (later known as Augustus) restored order to Rome following the civil wars of his father's time. He was a brilliant general and politician, and in 31-30 BCE he defeated the rebellious general Anthony, and Cleopatra, queen of Egypt.

GALLEYS

Roman warships, known as galleys, were propelled by a combination of sail and oar, with slaves as oarsmen. They had a huge battering ram on the bow to ram enemy ships. Although siege engines were sometimes mounted on deck, Roman ships were mostly used to transport troops or act as mere fighting platforms.

HANNIBAL

Rome's second attempt to invade Carthage was thwarted by Hannibal, a brilliant general who marched his army with forty war elephants across northern Africa, Spain, and across the Alps to Italy, to launch a surprise attack on Rome itself. Initially, Hanniba enjoyed some success but was eventually beaten in 202 BCE.

PRIDE OF ROME

Roman legions consisted of about 5,000 infantrymen and were the pride of the empire's army. They were supplemented by auxiliary cavalry who covered their flanks in an attack and scouted ahead, and by ordinary foot-soldiers, whose job it was to man the frontier forts protecting the empire from attack or rebellion. In command of each legion was a centurion who wore a distinctive helmet, such as this one, complete with crests or plumes, so he could be easily seen and followed in battle. Legionnaires were well-equipped and highly trained. They are believed to be the first army in history to be paid regular wages as a proper occupation.

LEGIONNAIRES

It is generally accepted that the success of the Roman Empire lay with its highly disciplined fighting legions. Earlier civilizations, including the Greeks and the Etruscans before them, proved incapable of raising and maintaining a centrally organized army. This severely limited their ability at sustained or widespread conquest. Without a standing army new colonies soon collapsed. By contrast, wherever the Romans conquered they left behind a strong military presence to consolidate their gains.

JULIUS CAESAR

Civil war frequently broke out in the "old" republic of Rome as generals competed for power. Julius Caesar (c.100-44 BCE) declared himself supreme dictator, but he was assassinated by his fellow senators who found he had become too powerful.

ROMAN WEAPONS

Roman weapons were usually made of iron or steel, with wooden or bone hand grips. Legionnaires were usually armed with a dagger and a sword. They favored short-bladed swords with double-edged blades, used as a stabbing weapon. Foot soldiers also used throwing spears, short bows and javelins, hurling them en masse into their enemy's midst.

SIEGE ENGINES

The most common form of Roman siege weapon was the *ballista*, as shown here. This impressive piece of military equipment could hurl a large boulder several hundred feet. They were also used to throw burning sticks and straw amongst enemy ships.

Crime & Punishment

The center of Roman lawmaking was the Senate in Rome itself, where members, known as senators, were voted into office and decisions of government arrived at after lengthy discussion. The system was open to abuse, however, and laws tended to be made, or repealed, more to appease public popularity than necessarily to be fair. The Romans first introduced the idea of magistrates' courts where crimes and grievances were heard. Punishment very often took the form of compensation rather than retribution and there were few prisons. Criminals sometimes had their sentences commuted to slavery, even if they were Roman citizens. Even offences against one of the many gods might have been considered a crime. Each city had an elected council of about 100 men, who usually held office for life.

THE NEW REPUBLIC

Following the chaos of civil war, which had led to the assassination of Julius Caesar, it fell upon his adopted son, Augustus, to restore order. Fortunately, he proved to be an able politician who carried out many reforms. He declared Rome a "new" republic and himself its first emperor.

CRUCIFIXION

Crucifixion was a common form of execution in Roman times and was not, as many suppose, reserved for religious victims. Death was slow and excruciatingly painful. Usually the victim's arms were tied above his head onto a single pole, sometimes they were fastened to a cross with their arms outstretched. Either way, the lungs gradually collapsed, causing death by asphyxiation.

CORRUPTION

The Romans took pride in having one of the fairest and most democratic constitutions of any nation in the known world. However, the system was open to abuse. The Senate was frequently the subject of corruption charges, leading to military unrest and civil war as powerful generals tried to seize control. As the power of Rome began to fade and economic chaos set in, many senators fell victim to bribery by rich merchants.

TRIAL BY COMBAT

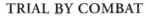

Many of those who were called upon to do battle in the Colosseum (as shown above) were criminals or religious martyrs. It amused the people to see such victims compete against wild animals or ruthless gladiators in an effort to gain their freedom. Even if they survived, many were trained to become gladiators themselves, living under the constant threat of death in the arena.

THE PRICE OF HOMAGE

The relief on this coin shows Augustus receiving a child from a barbarian. It was customary for emperors, following a great victory, to be presented with captured offspring in homage. Many conquered people became slaves; any who refused to pay homage were executed. Captured leaders were often executed by strangulation to serve as an example to newly conquered people.

DEATH BY EXECUTION

The Romans ruled their empire by might and oppression. Many crimes carried the death sentence, including stealing and treason. The methods of execution were equally varied. This illustration shows some of them; death by sword, axe and stoning.

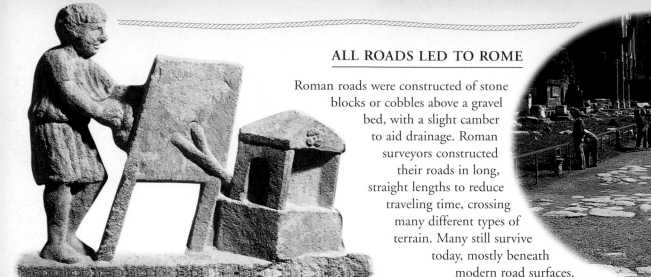

ALL ROADS LED TO ROME

Roman roads were constructed of stone blocks or cobbles above a gravel bed, with a slight camber to aid drainage. Roman surveyors constructed their roads in long, straight lengths to reduce traveling time, crossing many different types of terrain. Many still survive today, mostly beneath modern road surfaces.

SKILL WITH METALS

The Romans were skilled metalworkers, making tools, weapons, utensils, and intricate jewelry. They could not perfect the technique of smelting iron, so they heated solid pieces and hammered it into shape (forging). They made several alloys, including bronze (copper and tin) to which they added zinc to resemble gold.

HUMAN POWER

Sailing in Roman times was still a dangerous enterprise and usually undertaken only in good weather. Navigation was crude and relied on simple observation and plotting movements of the moon, stars and planets. The cargo ship shown in this mosaic would have been wind-powered (the mast is lowered), but supplementary power would have been provided by slave oarsmen for extra propulsion in calm weather.

LIGHTHOUSES

The ruin of this Roman pharos (lighthouse) can still be seen on the cliffs at Dover Castle, Kent. Originally, an identical structure stood on the opposite cliff. Lights were kept burning in the top tiers to guide ships into harbor.

ROAD TRANSPORT

Merchants used either pack animals or carts, pulled by oxen or horses, to transport their goods to market. Chariots, small two-wheeled carts pulled by up to four horses harnessed abreast, were only used for warfare and later specially adapted for racing.

Transport & Science

The Romans admired many of the achievements of the Greeks, particularly in art and architecture, and often emulated their styles. However, they used Greece more as a source of inspiration rather than copying them directly. The Romans went on to introduce and develop many of their own innovations, particularly in the advancement

of technology. They recognized the importance of a clean water supply to good health and so perfected a system of piping and drainage in their towns and villas. This lead to the development of plunge baths, and the invention of the hypocaust, their ingenious underfloor central heating system. In architecture they invented a new form of very strong concrete and improved the way bricks were manufactured. The Romans' use of arches allowed them to span greater distances than previous civilizations had been able to achieve and led to the invention of the dome. In glassmaking, they developed the new technique of glass-blowing, which made more intricate shapes possible. But perhaps the greatest success of the Roman Empire was the network of roads they constructed to facilitate rapid movement of soldiers and supplies.

ALL MOD CONS

This view shows the ruins of the Roman baths at Carthage, built between 145-162 CE. It clearly shows the hypocaust, where the floor was raised on pillars to allow the passage of hot air from adjoining furnaces. Grills in the floor above allowed the hot air to rise and heat the rooms.

CENTRAL HEATING

The hypocaust was a system of central heating based upon the principle that hot air rises. It both heated the water and warmed the rooms of private houses and public baths. This view shows how the system worked. Hypocausts were particularly popular in houses in the north, where it was colder in the winter.

Religion

Many of the gods in the Roman world were borrowed from ancient Greek mythology. The Romans renamed them, but also had a very different attitude towards them. Whereas the Greeks gave their gods a human familiarity, the Romans were a far more superstitious people, who lived in fear of their gods and made votive offerings to ward off evil spirits. They were also not averse to accumulating the gods and religious beliefs of the peoples they conquered, adding them to their own rich montage of beliefs. Romans posted to the outlying regions of the empire, such as Celtic Britain, frequently adopted their customs. Gradually, some Romans began to embrace Christianity, frequently worshipping the Christian God alongside their own. By about 337 CE Christianity had become the main religion of the Roman Empire.

PIVS SEXTVS P·M·REST·

APOLLO

Unlike all the other gods, Apollo was known by the same name to both the Greeks and Romans. He was the god of the sun and considered the most benevolent of all gods.

MITHRAISM

Mithras was originally the Persian god of light, identified with the sun. Here we see him slaying a bull in ritual sacrifice, to fertilize the world with its blood. Many soldiers in the Roman army adopted Mithraism as their religion.

GOD OF WAR

Mars was the Roman god of war and is usually depicted as a powerful soldier clad in full armor. The month of March is named in honor of him. He was the second most powerful god, after Jupiter. He is also associated with agriculture and many of his festivals were linked to the rural calendar, particularly spring and autumn.

KINGS OF THE GODS

The most powerful of all the Roman gods was Jupiter, who was said to have resided on the Capitol Hill in Rome itself, overseeing the honor of the empire. He was the god of light and the sky, symbolized by thunder and the eagle.

FEMALE CULTS

A few Roman religions were associated almost exclusively with women and fertility, such as Cybele, Isis and Vesta. This view shows the temple of Vesta, in Rome.

CATACOMBS

Although early Roman Christians may have used catacombs as a secret meeting place, their original purpose was as a place of burial, the bodies being placed in niches in the walls. The rock-hewn tunnel in this view leads to the shrine of the Sybil at Cumae. The Sybil was a devotee of Apollo, endowed by him with the gift of prophecy.

GODDESS OF WISDOM

The Roman goddess Minerva equates to the Greek Athena and was the goddess of handicrafts and wisdom. She is often depicted in a warlike stance to symbolize the power of the empire and adopted by the army to decorate their shields and armor. Britannia, who came to represent Britain, is thought to be based on her.

SACRIFICES

Sacrificial altars, although considered essential to many Roman religions, were generally placed outside the entrances to temples. A statue of the relevant god was placed inside.

Legacy of the Past

When studying the remains of Roman society today it is easy to get a false impression of what life was like. Almost all of the remains are of the impressive stone buildings, especially civic buildings, temples and villas, because these have better endured the passage of time. Although Roman society as a whole was rich and technologically brilliant, only the elite few enjoyed a luxurious lifestyle and we should temper our impression of their civilization by trying to imagine what life might have been like for ordinary people. However, there is no doubt that the Roman Empire left a legacy which has lasted right up to the present day. Many European roads are built over old Roman roads. Modern plumbing and sewerage systems owe much to the Romans; as does Western architecture and language. Other facets of their society, such as literature, military strategy and law, still influence us today.

ROAD BUILDING

Perhaps the greatest legacy left behind by the Romans was their engineering skills, particularly in road making. Many roads in Europe were not improved until the 19th century and often follow their original Roman course.

CLASSIC DESIGNS

Few Roman buildings survive anywhere in their entirety, but they have served as a source of inspiration to builders down the ages. In the 11th and 12th centuries, Norman architects emulated their style (now known as Romanesque) and in 18th- and 19th-century Britain architects borrowed many classical designs for their buildings.

THE EMPIRE DIVIDES

In 395 CE, the Roman Empire was divided into two states, east and west. By 476, the Western Empire had fallen to invaders from the north and become fully Christianized. The Eastern Empire remained virtually intact for another 1,000 years, calling itself Byzantium. Many of the Roman traditions prevailed including architectural styles, as this mausoleum shows.

THE FALL OF THE EMPIRE

In 406 CE, Germanic tribes overran the Rhine border in the north and in 410, Rome itself was sacked. The army was called back to defend Rome from the furthest outposts, including Britain. By 476 the Western Empire had fallen.

ATTILA THE HUN (*C.*406-53 CE)

The Roman Empire reached its zenith around 200 CE after which time it began to break up. There was continuous civil war at home and the empire was under constant attack along its many borders, particularly from the Persians in the east, and the Germanic tribes of the north. Chief among these were the Huns from central Asia. Attila the Hun was a ruthless warrior, known as the "scourge of god." He extended his territory from the Rhine to China and in 447 CE defeated the Roman emperor Theodosius.

THE STATES OF MODERN EUROPE

The break up of the Roman Empire was largely responsible for the formation of modern Europe. In the north, Franks settled in what is now France and the Saxons invaded England. In the east, Turkey retained elements of both east and west, as it still does. This view shows St Sophia Mosque in Istanbul.

UNIQUE SURVIVAL

The excavated city of Pompeii is a unique record of the Roman world. In 79 CE the city, located near present-day Naples, was destroyed (along with the neighboring town of Herculaneum) when the volcano Vesuvius suddenly erupted. For 1700 years the city and its people lay buried beneath the ash. Modern excavations have revealed a city virtually untouched by time, showing all aspects of everyday life for rich and poor alike.

Who were the Vikings?

The very word "Viking" conjures up images of fierce, uncivilized warriors and pirates who attacked and wrought havoc on the Christian countries of Europe from the 8th to the 11th century, but they are a much misunderstood people and it is not easy to unravel the truth from legend. To begin with, they were not peoples from one land, but three: Denmark, Norway and Sweden, coming from an area of northern Europe now known as Scandinavia. However, there was no unity and wars among these three Viking peoples were common. The word "Viking" is a general term (possibly derived from the word "*vik,*" which means "creek") to describe all Scandinavians of this time. They were also known as Norsemen (meaning men from the North), pagans, "ashmen" (after the preferred wood of their ships) and a range of other names. Although they did lead piratical raids against the Christian countries of Europe, the Vikings were not uncivilized barbarians. They were excellent navigators,and great traders, and they were skilled in the arts of metalwork and carpentry.

EXPERT NAVIGATORS

The Vikings were expert seamen. They used large, low-sided boats called longships. They were very sleek, fast vessels, propelled by a combination of a central sail and oars. Each oarsman hung his shield over the side as protection from attack.

RUNIC WRITING

The Vikings developed a form of writing called runes. Some of the letters were based on Roman ones, while others were invented to make easy shapes to cut into wood. Runes were also inscribed onto special stones, along with pictograms, and were used in religious rituals. Most Vikings would not have been able to read and write but they had a rich tradition of storytelling, especially epic poetry and heroic sagas.

MAP OF THE VIKING WORLD

The Vikings did not usually conquer countries with the intent of ruling them, but preferred simply to colonize lands of their choosing. Their domains were centered on Scandinavia, western Russia, England, Scotland, Ireland, northern France, the Faroe Islands, Iceland and Greenland. They also established a settlement in North America at Newfoundland for a short period around the year 1000 CE.

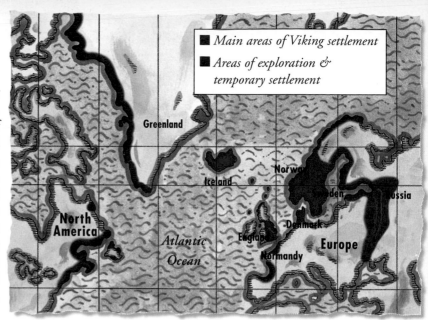

■ *Main areas of Viking settlement*
■ *Areas of exploration & temporary settlement*

Greenland

Norway

Iceland

Sweden

Russia

North America

Atlantic Ocean

Denmark

England

Normandy

Europe

WARRIOR RACE

Viking warriors were amongst the fiercest (and most feared) ever known. Most of their attacks took the form of raids using hit-and-run tactics. Coastal towns were most vulnerable, as were remote and isolated monasteries such as Lindisfarne in Northumberland, England, rich in gold and treasures, which the Vikings freely plundered. Gradually, they established semi-permanent bases from which to launch attacks further inland.

SIGN OF PRESTIGE

This solid silver armband shows how skilled Vikings were as metalworkers. Both men and women loved to wear decorative jewelry such as brooches, armbands, rings and necklaces. Wearing fine jewelry was an outward sign of a person's wealth.

SUPERSTITION

The Vikings worshiped many gods. These gods were given human personalities, and Norse mythology is rich in tales of their heroic deeds. This small bronze statuette dates from about 1000 CE and shows Frey, god of fertility.

Life for the Rich

Viking society was, in general, quite liberated. Although wealth and status could be inherited (usually from father to eldest son) it was also possible for warriors of quite lowly status to rise up the social scale simply by acquiring money and treasure on raiding expeditions. Such behavior was perfectly acceptable to the Vikings. Also, unlike the rich in other societies, wealthy Vikings continued to take part in expeditions, equipping themselves with fine armor and weapons. Wealthy Vikings often employed slaves (usually captured on raids) to do the menial work around the house and on the land. The typical home of a rich Viking was a large, timbered hall where the entire household lived, ate and slept together. Many, who had acquired their wealth by stealing from foreign lands, buried their treasure in secret hiding places rather than risk having it stolen from them. These hoards are still being unearthed today and can tell us much about Viking society.

STATUS SYMBOL

This beautiful silver disc brooch from Norway would probably have been used to fasten a chieftain's cloak at the shoulder. Fine jewelry showed a Viking's wealth as well as their status.

FINE WEAPONS

A Viking's position in society could be told as much by the quality of his weapons as by the cut of his clothes. The pride of every Viking warrior was his sword. They were usually made of iron, but with decorative inlays of silver, brass or even gold on the hilts (handles). The more wealthy the warrior, the more valuable his sword.

HIDDEN TREASURE

Wealthy Vikings often acquired many valuable objects, but they did not keep them on open display, as is the modern custom. Instead, they locked their valuables away inside strong wooden chests, such as this one made from oak with iron fittings. It was often the woman's responsibility to look after the chest, usually wearing the key as a sign of status. Anyone caught stealing from a locked chest was severely punished.

BURIALS

Vikings believed in an afterlife and were often buried with familiar objects and valuables in preparation for their journey after death. Some wealthy Vikings were buried with their ships and it is from their rediscovery by modern archeologists that we have learned so much about Viking life. Sometimes the ships were buried within mounds, while others were set on fire. If some were cast adrift and then set on fire, as depicted in this imaginative view, nothing remains for archeologists to find.

VIKING HALLS

Viking aristocrats and kings built large and elaborate wooden halls in which to house themselves and hold court with feasting and rich display. Their carpenters were excellent craftsmen, who had inherited woodworking skills developed by their ancestors over many centuries. They were capable of erecting impressive aisled buildings such as this 10th-century Danish structure with its roof of wooden shingles.

ACQUIRED WEALTH

Many of the most valuable items in a wealthy Viking's house were stolen during raids to other lands. This silver cup, found in Denmark, may have come originally from a Christian monastery. Vikings were skilled metalworkers in their own right, though only the rich could afford to buy such items.

HOME COMFORTS

This reconstruction at the Jorvik Viking Center in York, England (*above*) shows the interior of a typical Viking Age house. There was only one main room, where the entire family lived, ate and slept. In the center was an open fire where they cooked their food. The smoke simply seeped through the roof. Furniture would have been minimal, probably consisting of a table, stools, chests and beds only. Cooking was mainly done in earthenware pots like the one below

HOME FROM HOME

The Vikings used whatever materials were freely to hand to build their houses. They felt most comfortable with wood, but this was not always available. In the Scottish islands, such as the Shetlands and Orkneys, where there is virtually no tree cover, houses were constructed of the loose boulders that lay everywhere across the landscape. Unmortared walls were usually very thick to keep out the north winds, with turf or thatch roofs, and a few window openings. Some more modern farmhouses in Shetland (*above*) are still built in this way. In England, houses were made of upright wooden posts (staves) with thatched roofs; in Iceland, walls were sometimes made of turf blocks.

MEASURE OF WEALTH

Viking farmers relied on grazing animals for much of their food, including sheep, cattle, pigs, and even reindeer. In summer, animals might have been driven to higher pastures that would have been too inhospitable during the long winter months. Since land could not be freely bought and sold, the measure of a man's wealth was often made in the number of animals he kept.

Everyday Life

Viking society was divided into three main classes: slaves, freemen, and nobles, known respectively as thralls, karls, and jarls. Many of the slaves were captured in raids to foreign lands, while others became slaves through bad debt or crime. Much of the menial work was done by slaves and they had few rights. At the other end of the scale were nobles, who were few in number, but controlled large areas as overlords, responsible to the king. In between were freemen, whose ranks included farmers, traders, craftsmen and warriors. The vast majority of people were freemen. They mostly farmed their own land, but strict inheritance laws meant land was always scarce. Land was held in tenure and could not normally be sold or given away. It passed from father to eldest son, which meant any other sons had to seek their own land. It was this need for more land, especially amongst the poor, that first drove the Vikings to seize property abroad.

FARMING LIFE

Most Vikings were full-time farmers and only part-time warriors, and tending the farm was a family affair. In Scandinavia, much of the land was either forested or mountainous, making it difficult to farm, and the northerly latitude of the Viking homelands meant that the growing season was short. The search for better lands enticed Vikings to settle overseas.

MILITARY SERVICE

Military service took several forms in Viking society. Sometimes people helped to build camps like the one on the right as a form of service. In addition, everyone was expected to fight for their king or local chieftain when necessary, although there was no organized army. Most warriors were poor farmers who joined raiding expeditions to gain land, or a share in any treasure seized, to improve their situation.

Food & Drink

A DELICACY

Most Vikings lived close to the coast, where there were large colonies of sea birds, such as black-headed gulls (shown here). They roasted the birds and also gathered their eggs, which were considered a great delicacy. Ducks and geese were also eaten.

Most Vikings ate reasonably well. Although they mostly lived a subsistence form of existence on individual family-run farms, food was seldom in short supply. When crops failed or a family fell onto hard times, there was an abundance of wildlife to be hunted, including birds, rabbits, and deer. Vikings were opportunist hunters so when crops failed, most could gather what they needed to survive from the wild. Although they did not live in a classless society, there were fewer divisions between rich and poor; both rich and poor ate basically the same foods, the rich simply ate better, with more variety. Meat featured strongly in the Viking diet, as did fish. Vegetables, such as cabbages, beans, garlic, and peas were mostly used to make stews. Knives were usually the only implement used at table. Beer made from barley was the most common drink, though the wealthy often imported wine from Germany.

ABUNDANT SEAS

Not surprisingly for a seafaring people, fish formed an essential part of the Viking diet, including herring, haddock, trout and cod (*shown here*). Fish was available throughout the year and was either grilled or smoked. Fish oil was also used as a supplement.

FIT FOR A KING

This picture shows a typical banquet scene in a noble household in the 11th century. Several courses were served in finely decorated metal dishes. Meals were eaten in the communal great hall with the chieftain and his family sitting at the head table.

SHEPHERDS

The Vikings farmed several breeds of hardy sheep and goats able to cope with harsh terrain and the cold, northern climate. They provided a range of vital products, including wool (used for spinning and weaving), meat, and milk.

HARDY BREEDS

Vikings farmed several types of animal, including sheep, pigs, geese, deer, horses, poultry, and cows. They were kept for both food and materials (such as their hides and bones). The cow shown here is a longhorn, now a rare breed. Farm animals then were considerably smaller than many breeds today. They were also much more hardy and able to survive harsh conditions. Cattle were also used for pulling the plow in arable fields. At the onset of winter, when fodder was particularly scarce, many animals were slaughtered in an annual cull. Meat was preserved by salting down. The salt was acquired by laboriously boiling sea water in flat pans. As the water evaporated a thin salty deposit was left in the pan.

SKIN & BONE

Deer meat (venison) was sometimes an important part of the Viking diet. Elk, red deer, and reindeer all lived wild in herds throughout the Viking world, although sometimes they were farmed like sheep. The skins were used to make clothing and blankets; the bones and antlers for making tools, combs and decorative ornaments.

Pastimes

BOARD GAMES

Board games were very popular with Vikings, since many games of skill were based on the themes of war or capture. Particular favorites included the game of "hnefetafl," in which one player uses his pieces on a board to protect his king from an opponent's attacking pieces. The "hnefi," or "king" piece, is usually more elaborate than all the others. An opponent's pieces might be made of different materials, such as stone and bone, or colored differently to distinguish them.

Vikings were used to hard work, but they knew how to relax. When the day's work was done (be it toiling in the fields or soldiering) the evenings were often reserved for feasting. A great sense of community existed in the Viking world and often the whole village would congregate at the chieftain's hall for an evening of eating, drinking and entertainment. After the meal, epic poems about legendary heroes or stories of the gods were recited aloud (mostly from memory, although the nobles employed professional poets called skalds), and the whole community joined in with the rousing song and dance. Later in the evening, the behavior probably became more riotous. Other popular pastimes were combat sports such as wrestling.

Tuning peg

Bone whistle

SONG & DANCE

Music, dancing and singing featured strongly in Viking entertainment. In ordinary households songs were sung by the family. Richer people sometimes employed the services of professional musicians and singers to perform at special banquets. Shown here are a tuning peg from a stringed instrument such as a harp or lyre; the wooden bridge of a lyre; a bone whistle; and a slab of boxwood which has been made into a set of panpipes.

Bridge

Panpipes

A FEASTING WE WILL GO

Feasts and festivals were a popular form of entertainment, and a way for the rich to display their status and generosity. Sometimes held in honor of the gods or for a great warrior, they were probably also held to celebrate the return of a raiding party, when the spoils were shared out. Feasts were usually held in the chieftain's hall but were not exclusive. All members of the community were welcome to attend.

EQUESTRIAN SKILLS

Some Vikings were great horsemen, although they did not go into battle on horseback. Riding a fine horse with an elaborate saddle, horse-trappings and stirrups was a sign of high rank. This silver pendant of a horseman from Sweden dates from the 10th century.

HUNTING

Many of the Vikings' outdoor pursuits were as much a test of a warrior's bravery as they were pastimes. Hunting was a popular activity, especially pursuing dangerous animals such as bears. Warriors would often hunt on foot to prove their courage. Many Viking sports would be considered cruel by today's standards.

WINTER GAMES

During the long winter months, many Vikings enjoyed outdoor sports, such as skiing and sledding. They also went skating on the frozen lakes and rivers using ice skates made from the foot bones of cattle or horses.

FOOT LOOSE

Shoes were made of leather, using a wooden shoe-last to help fashion their shape. There were several common styles. Some shoes were secured by a strap and toggle, while others were slip-ons. Laces were never used on Viking shoes.

WOOLLEN CAPE

Capes were made of thick wool, often brightly colored using vegetable dye. Sometimes they were embroidered or had fur trims.

HEADDRESS

Women wore headbands or linen bonnets; men wore woollen caps. In the winter both men and women wore fur-lined hats and gloves.

NATURAL FIBERS

Most clothes were made from wool or linen (fibers extracted from the crushed stems of the flax plant). Materials were thick and closely woven to give maximum warmth. Some quite intricate patterns were woven into the cloth. Common patterns were checks, similar to Scottish tartans, and geometric shapes. Sometimes pictures, such as animal heads, were included in the design.

BODY WARMTH

Clothing was often loose fitting to allow circulation of air between layers (which preserves warmth), and held together with highly decorative pins, brooches and buckles.

Fashion

Viking clothing styles were generally unsophisticated, with the emphasis placed on warmth and comfort rather than style. They were not a particularly fashion-conscious people, except as a means of showing one's position in society. Silver and gold jewelry, for instance, was often imported, worn by the rich as a kind of status symbol. They wore their clothes in layers to fend off the cold. Both rich and poor wore more or less the same style of clothes; the rich simply used better quality materials, sometimes even imported silks. For most Vikings clothes were purely functional, with few concessions to decoration. On special occasions wealthy Vikings might wear more elaborately embroidered tunics, perhaps with fur trims.

BELTING UP

Leather belts were used to hold clothes at the waist, or to support weapons. Buckles were usually molded from metal, highly embossed or engraved for decoration. This belt end was made from carved bone.

BEADS & BROOCHES

The richly decorated brooch (*right*) would probably have held together the cape of a nobleman. The beads were from a simple amber necklace.

UNDERGARMENTS

Men wore knee-length tunics with woollen leggings beneath. Linen undergarments were also worn. Women wore ankle-length linen under-dresses, often with a pinafore-style over-dress on top.

Art & Architecture

The Viking homelands of Denmark, Norway and Sweden were thickly forested, so it is perhaps not surprising that Vikings chose to build with timber in preference to stone. Sadly, because of the vulnerability of wood to fire and damp, only remnants survive of their buildings and ornately carved woodwork, but it is enough to form a picture of their carpentry skills and artistry. Although no wooden churches survive from the main period of Viking activity (between the 8th and 11th centuries), several churches from the succeeding centuries of the medieval period do still stand, and they give us a good idea of what Viking buildings were like. The Vikings also produced finely crafted metalwork, but perhaps their greatest artistic legacy is in the carved stones they left behind, which used a combination of runes and pictograms. Many of these have religious significance, or tell stories from Nordic mythology, while others are memorial stones, dedicated to the deeds of fallen warriors.

MEMORIAL STONES

Elaborately-carved memorial stones are a striking feature of Viking art. They usually tell of heroic deeds performed by warriors. They were not placed on tombs, however, but in public places in celebration of the dead.

JEWELER'S ART

This magical amulet was worn on the chest, suspended from the neck on a chain, and was probably worn to ward off evil spirits. It shows how highly skilled the Vikings were at working metal into intricate shapes or molding pieces using molten metal. However, most jewelry was made for practical purposes, like brooches and dress pins used to hold items of clothing in place.

VIKING HALLS

Building farmhouses was a family affair which called upon the traditional techniques and methods that had been handed down over generations. Raw materials vary from place to place, but were most commonly timber, stone rubble and turf, with thatch roofs. This is the reconstructed farmhouse of a prosperous Viking Age farmer from Denmark.

STAVE CHURCH

Following their conversion to Christianity around 960–1000 CE, Viking kings and landowners erected many wooden churches throughout Scandinavia. They built them in the same unique and distinctive style as their halls and houses, with elaborately carved wooden staves (planks or logs) set upright into the ground. Roofs were made of wooden tiles.

DOMESTIC ARCHITECTURE

Most ordinary people lived in small houses constructed of timber. As well as being easily available, timber was often warmer than stone in the cold Scandinavian climate. Inside, the floors were simply beaten dirt, and furniture would have been minimal. Space had to be allowed for a loom, as shown above.

CARVING

Viking craftsmen never missed an opportunity to carve wood into elaborate designs, often depicting heroic exploits of warriors or scenes from mythology. This 12th century example comes from a stave church in Norway, and shows a continuation of the love of complex interlace patterns that were so common in the Viking Age.

Health & Medicine

With no understanding of how the body worked, no idea of surgery, and no concept of hygiene, Vikings suffered greatly (and often died) from conditions which today would be quickly cured. To avoid illness, people might carry lucky charms or amulets which they believed offered protection against disease. In case of illness, there were few ways to seek a remedy. One involved the use of charms or chants, or patterns of ritual behavior, begging the gods for relief. More practically, there was a substantial inherited wisdom about the benefits which various natural remedies were believed to provide. Some plant extracts were indeed beneficial, but others were completely useless as well as tasting revolting.

DIVINE INTERVENTION

Much of Viking medicine was still firmly rooted in religious divination. This wood carving from a stave church shows the mythical Sigurd divining the heart of a dragon, seeking answers from the gods by magical means. Such methods of diagnosis were commonly used in medicine.

IN THE LAP OF THE GODS

Illness was often thought of as a punishment from the gods. Good health could be assured by pleasing them. Frey, and his sister Freyja (*shown left*), were gods of fertility, love and birth. To ensure a healthy baby, pregnant women made offerings at their shrines.

HERBAL CURES

Most Viking medicine took the form of herbal remedies using the plants that were readily available from the land. Common herbal cures in general use were red clover (*shown right*—to purify the blood), nettles (to improve the circulation), stinking arrach (to cure ulcers), eyebright (to cure eye infections), willow bark (to treat rheumatism brought on by the damp), and viper's bugloss (to treat snake bites).

SKULLSPLITTER

Injuries suffered in battle were an occupational hazard for a Viking and sometimes had fatal consequences. Nothing could be done to save someone who was unable to defend himself against a sword blow to the head such as this, which has almost cut the skull in two.

HEALTHY LIFESTYLE

This face from the Viking Age has been reconstructed using computer modeling techniques. It is based upon a skull excavated in York. Vikings would have looked much like modern Europeans, but they had a much shorter life expectancy. Because of the dangers of childbirth (*see below*) women on average lived to just 35. Men, however, frequently survived into their 50s.

THE DANGERS OF CHILDBIRTH

Birth and the year or so afterwards was a dangerous time for both the infant and its mother. Lack of nutrition and disease took their toll on bodies that were already weak or weakened, and resulted in a death rate which is enormously high when compared with modern times. Babies' bones, being very fragile, usually dissolve quickly in the soil, but here the tiny remains of a nine–month–old child can be seen resting on its mother's hip.

EMIGRATIONS

For many poorer Viking families scarcity of land meant that the wives could not remain at home while their husbands were away on raiding expeditions. Instead, they accompanied their husbands, taking their possessions and children with them to set up home in the new colonies, as this romantic 19th-century painting depicts.

MARRIAGE

In Scandinavian Viking Age society the family was an important unit in such crucial matters as status, wealth and inheritance. Marriage was therefore a serious matter, with family prestige as important as individual attraction; it was also an occasion for feasting and gifts. The dangers of everyday life meant that both men and women were often widowed and then re-married.

HEARTH & HOME

In Viking society, the family, or kindred, was all important. Any action or crime against one member of the family was, by custom, against the entire family, as shown in this romantic 19th-century illustration. The custom also provided a crude form of social security, because the kindred looked after a female member and her children should her husband die or be killed.

Love & Marriage

Despite the fact that Viking women were reasonably liberated, most marriages were arranged between both sets of parents. The marriage ceremony was divided into two stages. The first was the wedding, or 'pledging', when the two families would agree terms for the bride-price. The bride's family would then hand over the agreed dowry to the groom's family. The second stage was the gift, or 'giving-away', when the bride's father literally gave his daughter to the groom, followed by a feast paid for and held in the bride's father's house. Once married, Viking women acquired certain rights, including the right to hold their own land.

BRYNHILD

In Viking myth, Brynhild was a beautiful Viking Valkyrie, a female warrior and messenger to Odin, god of war. Valkyries have always captured the imagination of artists, as in this romantic 19th-century illustration.

MAINTENANCE PAYMENTS

Until Vikings converted to Christianity, women reserved the right to divorce their husbands whenever they chose. More often than not, they did so simply because their spouse was not a good provider. If a husband divorced his wife he was obliged to pay her compensation. If she left with the children she was entitled to half the husband's wealth.

Women & Children

Women in Viking society enjoyed a high degree of freedom. Although men were normally head of the family household, the women were independent-minded and strong-willed. When their husbands were away fighting on the many military campaigns, the running of the farms fell on women's shoulders. During such times they undertook all of the duties usually performed by the men. On occasions this might include taking up arms to fight. Although it is doubtful they took part in military attacks, they certainly helped the men defend Viking colonies when the need arose. The freedom enjoyed by Viking women even extended to attending the law-making assemblies (*Things*). Children did not attend school, but were expected to help with duties around the house and farm.

CONSOLIDATED GAINS

Women did not always stay at home while their husbands were away. Sometimes they accompanied them in the hope of acquiring land in one of the new colonies. They traveled with the men in the longships and sheltered somewhere safe until the fighting was over. This practice enabled the Vikings to establish strong footholds in other countries very quickly.

HOME-SPUN

One of the principal duties of Viking women (and some men) was to make clothes for the family. They were skilled spinners and weavers of wool and linen. Most households had an upright hand-loom (*shown left*) which simply leant against one wall of the house. Stones were used to weigh down the threads and keep them taut while the material was woven, employing some quite intricate designs.

A WARRIOR'S LIFE

From about the age of 12, boys began serious weapon training. Many went on raiding expeditions by the age of 16. There was no standing army, as such, but each man owed allegiance to his local chieftain and could be called upon to fight at any time. For boys and young men from poor families, going on Viking expeditions was the quickest way to amass wealth.

WELL-GROOMED

Viking women were proud of their appearance, especially their hair. Long hair was fashionable and women spent a great deal of time combing it. Combs were often made from antlers (*shown left*). The bone thread reels and spindle whorls, to the right, were used in spinning.

SURVIVAL OF THE FITTEST

Life in Viking society was hard. Weakness was not tolerated, not even in children. If a new-born baby was sickly and likely to be a liability for the family, the father reserved the right to expose it to the elements, or cast it into the sea, where it soon died.

War & Weaponry

Although the Vikings did settle in parts of Britain, Ireland, France and Russia on a permanent basis, they were not initially seeking to conquer these lands. They were opportunist pirates, certainly warlike, but not barbarians, as they are often depicted. They lived, for the most part, in an ordered society. Viking warriors, however, were feared throughout Europe for their ferocity. Viking warriors had no fear of death; if they died on the battlefield it was considered an honorable death.

To surrender or be taken prisoner would have brought shame and dishonor to their families. Vikings launched attacks by sailing within sight of land and then, often by cover of darkness, slipping unnoticed into river estuaries and creeks. This meant they could make surprise attacks on less protected villages further inland.

THE VALIANT WARRIOR

The valor with which Vikings fought was closely linked to their religious beliefs. They believed that fallen warriors were transported to Asgard, home of the gods, where they fought alongside Odin, the chief of the gods. Each night they would be healed of their injuries and would feast in the hall of Valhalla (Viking heaven). The harder a warrior fought in this world, the more he would be favored by the gods in the afterlife.

MENACING FIGUREHEADS

Vikings often carved menacing figureheads onto the bows of their ships and on the front of their sledges (*left*) to strike fear into the hearts of their enemies on approach, or to protect themselves from evil. The figures might be mythical monsters, such as dragon heads, or representations of fierce warriors. The Vikings were a superstitious race and sometimes they carved the likeness of a deity, such as Thor, as protection in battle.

WARRIOR'S HELMET

Although popular fiction usually depicts Vikings wearing helmets adorned with animal horns, they were in fact the exception and not the rule, very much reserved for ceremonial or religious occasions. The type of helmet worn by warriors was hornless. Often it had either a nose-plate or eye-guards for added protection, and sometimes a chain mail neck guard. It was usually made from iron plates welded together.

LONGSHIPS

Remains of Viking longships have been discovered in burial mounds and wrecks have also been found, deliberately sunk to block water channels. These discoveries have given us a good idea of what these ships looked like. They were well made, of clinker construction (overlapping boards to keep the water out), and varied in length from about 60–90 feet (18–27 meters), and from 10–17 feet (3–5 meters) wide. They had a prominent keel (base) and a shallow draught, which meant not much of the boat lay under water. This meant that longships could be landed with ease by beaching in narrow inlets, without the need for a quay.

FAVORITE WEAPONS

Swords were the favorite weapon of most Viking warriors and were treated as prize possessions. It was common for a warrior to be buried with his sword to take with him into the afterlife to continue the battle. In Scandinavian mythology, swords were endowed with magical powers and were given names such as "killer." Swords were usually single-handed but double-edged, and were made of iron. Other popular weapons were bow and arrows, and spears for both throwing and thrusting. The weapons shown here are a typical sword and a spear. Most warriors also carried a circular shield, made of wood with a central iron boss, sometimes fitted with a spike for thrusting at the enemy.

BATTLE-AXE

The battle-axe is the weapon most often associated with Viking warriors. It was in fact as common as the sword, because some axes could be used as tools and weapons. The axe heads were made of iron and were often highly decorated. The shafts were made of wood.

Crime & Punishment

DEATH BY SACRIFICE

Crimes such as theft, assault, or murder could be punished in several ways. Compensation payments from the guilty person to the victim or victim's family could wipe the slate clean, or sometimes the guilty were banished overseas. Alternatively, vengeance could be taken through a blood feud, with payback killings which might last for generations. Public killings, like the hanging shown on the far left of this picture stone from Lärbro parish on the Swedish island of Gotland, probably had religious overtones.

The Vikings were not as lawless as one might suppose. They actually operated a form of government that involved ordinary men in the law-making process. Unusually for the time, even the wives of chieftains and freemen were allowed to give their opinions. Most crimes were punishable by compensation, but if the victim or their family refused payment of money, they reserved the right to exact revenge upon the perpetrator of a crime or his family. A complex system of compensation existed for crimes ranging from theft, right through to murder. Trial by combat or by ordeal were also common, for Vikings believed the innocent would be protected by the gods. Each year at the annual assembly, the Law Speaker recited all the laws to ensure that everyone knew them.

EXTORTION

In the late 10th century, Viking kings, having consolidated their position at home, renewed their attacks on England with a vengeance. Sweyn, King of Denmark, inflicted havoc once more on English towns, and agreed to leave only on payment of a bribe, called Danegeld, exacted from the taxpayers. However, Sweyn had a habit of returning to conquered lands, and the English king Ethelred the Unready, was completely unable to resist the new invasion.

THE ALTHING

Once a year in Iceland, a national assembly met to make decisions of government. This was called the Althing. The main picture shows the meeting place in Iceland, called Thingvellir ("Parliament Plains"). It was the site of the first meeting in 930 CE.

THE THING

Vikings operated a fairly free and democratic society in which landowners and freemen had their say. Local chieftains ruled over small regions, but they were controlled by an assembly, called a Thing. Here every freeman had the right to have their say on all issues ranging from local disputes, compensation claims, and matters of government and law. One such assembly was at Tynwald Hill on the Isle of Man (a Viking colony), where the modern government of this island still meets annually.

TRAVELING FAR & WIDE

The Vikings traveled great distances in their search for land and treasure. Wherever possible, they did so by water. Some of their ships were comparatively light and easily transportable and could be carried short distances overland between rivers. They exploited much of western Russia this way, reaching as far south as the Mediterranean and even had contacts with the Middle East. This bronze figure of Buddha was brought back to Sweden along a trading network which extended to northern India. In the west they reached as far as North America.

YOUR CARRIAGE AWAITS

This Viking wagon is in the Oslo ship museum in Norway. It is heavily constructed from wood and is typical of the finest wagons used at that time. The upper carriage was, like so much else in the Viking world, heavily carved with mythical symbols. The wheels are interesting in that instead of being solid circles of wood (more usual for the time) they have a sturdy rim and spokes, giving maximum strength with less weight.

BRIDGING THE GAP

The Vikings were great bridge builders. Their mountainous terrain was criss-crossed with many watercourses, which made transport difficult. It was the responsibility of the local population to keep its bridges in good repair. Bridges were normally constructed from wood.

Transport & Technology

The Vikings were not always the uncultivated, blood-thirsty warriors that history has portrayed them as. Mostly they were farmers and settlers with a bold spirit of adventure, seeking out new lands, and were highly skilled metal and woodworkers. They were something of a "magpie" society in that, although they brought few new innovations to the countries they invaded and settled, they quickly adapted to the ways of their host nations and absorbed many of the ideas they encountered into their own way of life. The Vikings had a reasonably good network of roads (mostly in the form of tracks) and bridges, essential in the often inhospitable terrain of their northerly homelands. Bridges also assumed a religious significance and were often associated with the journey to the afterlife. Viking mythology contains many references to legendary heroes who protected bridges from attack.

TRADING PLACES

The Vikings were great traders, just as much as they were great pirates. They opened up many trade routes, exchanging amber, furs and animal skins for more exotic goods, such as silver and gold, silk, and jewels. Always astute businessmen, wherever they went Viking traders took finely-crafted scales with them, usually made of bronze and transported in specially made carrying cases.

CARGO BOATS

The Vikings were expert navigators and shipbuilders. The seas were uncharted so they found their way by the sun, stars, landmarks and other natural indicators. They used two main types of boat; longships for war, and knarrs for fishing and trading. Both were open, clinker-built (overlapping planks) and propelled by a combination of oars and a central square sail. They had strong keels (the backbone of a ship) that cut through the water easily, making them incredibly seaworthy. They were steered by a rudder or steering board on the right-hand side of the ship, from where the term "starboard" (meaning to the right of a ship) is derived.

SLEIGH RIDE

One of the principal means of getting around the frozen landscape in winter was by sled. The biggest were quite large, about the same size as a wagon, but with two wooden blades instead of wheels to enable speedy transport through the snow and ice. They were sometimes decorated with ornate wood carvings, like this one.

Religion

There were many different gods in Viking religion. Many began as simple nature spirits, but gradually evolved into a complex mythology, telling stories of heroic, warrior-like gods that reflected their own lifestyle. The three most important gods were Odin, Thor and Frey. Odin was chief of the gods and symbolized, amongst other things, war, courage and wisdom. Thor was the god of thunder, while Frey was the god of fertility. Vikings thought of their gods in much the same way as they viewed themselves, fighting against the powers of evil and darkness. Strangely, however, they also believed that they and their gods were fighting a lost cause, doomed to failure. It was this belief that was largely responsible for the heroism of Viking warriors, for by dying a hero's death on Earth they could join the gods in Valhalla, the Viking heaven, and continue the struggle there.

OLD & NEW

For many years the recently converted Vikings did not fully accept Christianity and continued to worship their old gods alongside the new faith. This amulet in the shape of Thor's hammer also incorporates Christian symbolism.

MISCHIEVOUS LOKI

Loki is a strange creature in Norse mythology, part-god and part-devil. He seems to have created mischief wherever he went and was an instigator of discord amongst the gods. He is often associated with fire and blacksmiths' forges. He is seen here on a forge stone with his lips sewn together having tried to trick a dwarf blacksmith.

120

CHRISTIANITY ARRIVES

The Vikings became influenced by Christianity on their raiding expeditions to lands in western Europe. King Harald Bluetooth converted Denmark to Christianity around 960 CE, and raised this stone at Jelling in Denmark to commemorate the event. Norway and Sweden were christianized half a century later. At first Christianity was seen simply as a way of strengthening ties with other Christian countries; tradesmen wearing crucifixes were usually allowed free passage. Canute of Denmark, who became king of England in 1016 CE, was a Christian who gave gifts to churches that had been ransacked or destroyed by his pagan ancestors.

THOR, GOD OF THUNDER

Thor is one of the great heroes of Viking mythology. He was the god of thunder and carried a mighty silver hammer possessed of magical powers. When he used it to strike an enemy, thunder was heard in the heavens. Thor rode through the sky in a magnificent chariot. He symbolized everything a good Viking warrior should strive to be.

ODIN

Odin was the most powerful of the Viking gods. He was often accompanied by a raven, a flesh-eating scavenger of battle-fields, and Odin was particularly associated with warfare. Here he has his foot in the mouth of a fierce wolf, Fenrir, who will swallow Odin at the end of the world. This scene is carved on a 10th-century cross-slab at Andreas, on the Isle of Man.

Legacy of the Past

The Vikings have left traces of their existence all over northern Europe, from Scandinavia to Britain. To some extent the strongest influence of the Vikings was not felt directly, but from the descendants of one of their colonies, the Normans, who had settled in an area of northern France known as Normandy. Under them, Europe suffered a further wave of invasions. The influence of the Normans was felt for several centuries afterwards and greatly influenced the political and cultural direction taken by most countries in medieval Europe. Perhaps the greatest legacy left behind by the Vikings, however, is their rich tapestry of mythology and epic poems, every bit as complex and colorful as that of the Greeks and Romans. Nordic stories and poems are among the finest works of literature to survive from the Dark Ages.

VIKING GRAVEYARD

The Viking-age cemetery at Lindhol Høje in Denmark contains almost 700 graves, many marked by triangular, oval or ship-shaped stone settings. It is one of the most extensive Viking cemeteries in the world, and looks like a fleet of stone ships. In the 11th century the graveyard was covered by drifting sand, preserving the site until this day.

DAYS OF THE WEEK

Several days of the week are named after Viking gods. Tuesday is named after Tyr, the Viking god of war *(shown above with a tethered animal)*. Wednesday is named after Woden (or Odin), while his wife, Freya (or Frigga), gave her name to Friday. Thursday is named after the thunder god, Thor.

UP-HELLY-AA

In parts of Britain, the Viking legacy is immediately apparent. Every year on January 29 in Lerwick, the capital of the Shetland Islands, a replica of a Viking ship is burned in the festival known as Up-Helly-Aa. The Shetland Islands, together with the Orkney Islands, belonged to Norway until 1469, and although Up-Helly-Aa and its Viking ship burning is not an ancient festival, the event is a fitting reminder of the area's strong Viking contacts.

AMERICAN SETTLEMENTS

A Viking base-camp, where ships were repaired and people overwintered in about 1000 CE, has been found at the north tip of Newfoundland, at L'Anse aux Meadows. This discovery shows that later stories about a land to the west of Greenland, which the Vikings called Vinland ("wineland"), are grounded in fact, and the Vikings did reach North America. The main buildings were reconstructed by archeologists after excavation.

THE NORMANS

In 911 CE a Norwegian prince called Rolf (or Rollo) invaded northern France with a Viking army consisting mainly of Danes. The French king, Charles the Simple, offered them an area of France in return for peace. This area became known as Normandy (land of the North, or Norsemen). The Treaty of St. Claire-sur-Epte gave Rolf a dukedom, subject to the French king. Rolf and his followers soon settled and adopted many French ways, eventually forming a powerful nation in their own right. This scene from the Bayeux tapestry shows the Norman conquest of England in the 11th century. Their boats show the direct influence of the Viking longships.

INDEX

DID YOU KNOW?

That the tombs of the pharaohs were protected by a curse? In order to protect the dead pharaohs and their possessions in their journey to the afterlife, their tombs were protected by a curse that said anyone who defiled their tombs would die. Coincidentally, following the discovery of Tutankhamun's tomb in 1922, several of those involved died violent deaths, including Lord Carnarvon, financier of the expedition, who died from an infected mosquito bite five months later. However, modern archeologists have detected traces of poisons painted onto the walls of tombs which may have aided the curse to come true!

That the word "platonic" is derived from the Greek philosopher Plato? Plato believed that it was possible for both men and women to forge deep non-sexual friendships, based entirely on spiritual ideas and nurtured by philosophical debate (Plato actually encouraged women students to take part in debates). Such friendships, sometimes the cause of jealousy and resentment between married couples, are still known as "platonic."

That Rome first introduced passports? To ensure the safe passage of merchants and political envoys within the empire and through foreign lands, the Romans issued a "certificate of safe conduct" which was shown to the ruler of each country passed through on a journey. The certificate carried the full protection of Rome and contained words of warning to any foreign official who did not honor it and allow the safe passage of its bearer.

That Norse mythology may have inspired Tolkien to write the Hobbit? Although the children's fantasy novel *The Hobbit*, and its epic sequel *The Lord of the Rings*, are works of pure fiction, their author, J.R.R. Tolkien, drew upon his intimate knowledge of Norse mythology when he created the Hobbits and the kingdom of Middle Earth. Dwarfs and runes figure prominently in the stories, as do several other Scandinavian elements, including place names and magic, all of which feature prominently in Viking myths.

That the term "going berserk" is derived from the Vikings? One of the Viking gods of war was Tyr. He is often depicted wearing a bear-skin cloak with the bear's head draped over his helmet. The Viking word for "bear-skin" was "berserk" and a special class of warrior, all dressed in bear-skins, came to be known as "berserkirs." They used to work themselves up into a rage before going into battle, from where the modern term "going berserk," is derived. The frenzy may have been drug-induced.

ACKNOWLEDGEMENTS

We would also like to thank: Graham Rich, Tracey Pennington, and Peter Done for their assistance.

ISBN 978 1 84696 831 0

Printed in China.

North American edition copyright © 2008 *ticktock* Entertainment Ltd.

First published in North America in 2008 by *ticktock* Media Ltd.

Unit 2, Orchard Business Centre, North Farm Road, Tunbridge Wells, Kent, TN2 3XF, U.K. All rights reserved.

No part of this publication may be reproduced, stored in a retrieval system, or transmitted in any form or by any means, electronic, mechanical, photocopying, recording or otherwise, without prior written permission of the copyright owner.

AKG: 29tr, 35cb, 36bl, 37br, 38-39cb, 39r, 39tl, 40-41c, 41tr, 42-43c, 44bl, 45br, 45t, 44-45ct, 49cl, 50bl, 50tl, 50-51c, 51tr, 54bl, 54br, 54-55c, 56bl, 57r, 58b, 58tl, 59tl, 60tr, 60bl, 72-73, 79br, 85t, 86bl, OBCr(b). Alinari /Giraudon, Paris: 69t, 71bc, 76bl, 81tr, 93br. John Alston: 98tr. Ancient Art and Architecture: 6tl, 12br, 13tr, 19br, 21br, 22-23ct, 23cr, 24tr, 25br, 26tl, 32tl, 80cl, 84-85, 85cb, 115cb, OBCl(a). Archives Larousse/Giraudon: 72-73bc. ATA Expedition: 116tl. Bridgeman Art Library: 78-79t, 79cr, 89br. Bridgeman/Giraudon: 109tr, 113br, 113-114t. CFCL/Image Select: 34tl, 59br, 62bl, 62tl, 98-99b, 101br. Graham Collins: 94-95c, 99tr, 103tr, 104-105c, 110-111c. Corbis Images: 99br, 109tr, 113cr. et archive: 9bl, 12-13c, 18-19ct, 24b, 30-31cb, 24-25, 108bl. Chris Fairclough Colour Library/Image Select: 4-5ct, 8bl, 16-17ct, 18cr, 68-69c, 77cr, 78tl, 82bl, 92-93c. Giraudon: 31tr, 34b, 36tl, 36tr, 37tr, 42tl, 43r, 44-45cb, 46tl, 46-47ct, 48r, 52-53cb, 53br, 53tr, 61br, 64tl, 64-65bc, 66c, 68tl, 68-69b, 70b, 70-71c, 74tl, 74-75b, 76tl, 77tl, 78b, 81b, 83tl, 83tr, 87t, 87b, 88tl, 88bl, 88-89c, 90c, 90-91b, 91tr, 92b, 106-107b, 122-123cb. Richard Hall: 96-97c, 106bl, 120-121c, 122tl, 123cr. Image Select: 2, 12bl, 15bl, 16tl, 23c, 29cr, 30c, 36-37c, 42c, 42-43cb, 52l, 52-53cb, 53cr, 54tr, 55tr, 60-61cb, 61cb, 62tr, 63br, 63tr, 64-65tc, 65br, 65tr, 67tr, 67b, 71tl, 72tl, 72tr, 74-75t, 74bl, 75br, 76-77b, 77br, 84tl, 90-91t, 91tc, 92-93c, 100-101b, 112bl, 128, OBCr(a), OBCl(b). Knudsens Fotosenter/Giraudon: 114bl, 119cb, OBCl(d). Ann Ronan at Image Select: 9r, 10t, 10cr, 15tr, 17c, 18l, 20-21c, 40c, 44tl, 48l, 49tr, 49tl, 51br, 53cl, 54tl, 55br, 56tl, 56-57c, 57tr, 59c, 59tr, 60tl, 61tr, 69c, 69r, 79tr, 79bl, 84cb, 85cr, 85br, 86tl, 88-89t, 88-89c, 90l, 91br, 93tr, 99b, 100tl, 100-101c, 100b, OBCr(c). Look and Learn/The Bridgeman Art Library: OFCb. Gilles Mermet/Giraudon: 80-81t, 84bl. National Maritime Museum, London: 33tl. National Museum of Denmark: 97bl, 121t. PIX: 4b, 5cl, 8-9c, 17tr, 17cl, 22tl, 22bl, 24tl, 25br, 26bl, 30-31ct, 33tr, 34-35c, 35c, 38tl, 38bl, 38r, 38-39cb, 39r, 40t, 41br, 42bl, 46-47 (main), 47tr, 49br, 92tl, 101tr, 106tl, 115tl, 118c. Roskilde Viking Ship Museum: 113t, 119cl. Shutterstock: OFCt, OFCc. Spectrum Colour Library: 22br, 29br, 32-33(main), 33cl, 62-63c, 63bl, 70tl, 117c. Charles Tait: 122-123t. Telegraph Colour Library UK: 40b, 92l. Universiteters Oldsaksamling Oslo: 96tl, 96-97cb, 115cl, 114-115ct, OBCr(d). Werner Forman Archive: 4tl, 5cr, 5br, 6bl, 7br, 7tr, 7c, 6-7c, 9tr, 10cl, 10bl, 10-11c, 11tr, 11br, 12tl, 12-13cb, 13br, 14br, 14l, 15br, 15cl, 15cr, 16b, 18-19cb, 19tr, 20tl, 20bl, 21c, 21tr, 25tr, 26-27c, 27t, 27b, 28tl, 28bl, 28-29c, 30l, 30r, 66tl, 66tr, 66b, 67c, 71r, 73tr, 75tr, 80cr, 80tl, 80bl, 82tl, 82-83b, 82-83c, 87c, 89tr, 91bc, 94bl, 95c, 95br, 98bl, 103cr, 105br, 105cb, 107br, 108bl, 109cr, 111br, 116-117t, 116-117(background), 118tl, 119tr, 120tl, 120bl, 121r, OBCl(c). York Archaeological Trust: 94tl, 98tl, 102tl, 102bl, 103br, 104bl, 104tl, 105tr, 104-105b, 107t, 108-109c, 109tl, 109br, 113cr, 116-117t.